50 Greece Ice Cream Recipes for Home

By: Kelly Johnson

Table of Contents

- Mastiha Ice Cream
- Greek Yogurt Ice Cream with Honey and Nuts
- Kaimaki Ice Cream
- Baklava Ice Cream
- Ouzo Ice Cream
- Lemon Basil Sorbet
- Feta Cheese Ice Cream
- Halva Ice Cream
- Loukoumi Ice Cream
- Metaxa Ice Cream
- Orange Blossom Ice Cream
- Olive Oil Ice Cream
- Pistachio Ice Cream
- Melomakarona Ice Cream
- Saffron Ice Cream
- Greek Coffee Ice Cream
- Rosewater Ice Cream
- Mastic and Almond Ice Cream
- Spiced Fig Ice Cream
- Grapefruit Mint Sorbet
- Mastelo Cheese Ice Cream
- Cinnamon Walnut Ice Cream
- Vanilla Tahini Ice Cream
- Pomegranate Sorbet
- Honey Lavender Ice Cream
- Raisin and Cinnamon Ice Cream
- Thyme Honey Ice Cream
- Greek Mountain Tea Ice Cream
- Lemon Chamomile Sorbet
- Plum and Anise Ice Cream
- Grape and Ouzo Sorbet
- Honey Baklava Ice Cream
- Cherry Mastelo Ice Cream
- Pistachio and Mastiha Ice Cream
- Greek Yogurt and Figs Ice Cream

- Cucumber Mint Sorbet
- Lemon Ouzo Ice Cream
- Melon Sorbet
- Apricot and Honey Ice Cream
- Rose Petal Ice Cream
- Watermelon Mint Sorbet
- Mastic Rose Ice Cream
- Almond and Honey Ice Cream
- Pear and Ginger Ice Cream
- Mastic Pistachio Ice Cream
- Olive Oil and Sea Salt Ice Cream
- Lemon Thyme Sorbet
- Lavender and Honey Ice Cream
- Greek Yogurt and Honey Sorbet
- Mastelo and Cinnamon Ice Cream

Mastiha Ice Cream

Ingredients:

- 2 cups whole milk
- 1 cup heavy cream
- 3/4 cup sugar
- 1 teaspoon mastiha (mastic) resin, ground into a powder
- 4 egg yolks
- 1 teaspoon vanilla extract

Instructions:

1. **Heat the Milk and Cream:**
    - In a medium saucepan, combine the whole milk and heavy cream. Heat the mixture over medium heat until it begins to steam, but do not let it boil.
2. **Add the Sugar and Mastiha:**
    - Gradually add the sugar and ground mastiha to the hot milk and cream mixture, stirring continuously until the sugar and mastiha are completely dissolved.
3. **Prepare the Egg Yolks:**
    - In a separate bowl, whisk the egg yolks until they become thick and pale in color.
4. **Temper the Egg Yolks:**
    - Slowly add a small amount of the hot milk and cream mixture to the egg yolks, whisking constantly to prevent the eggs from curdling. Continue adding the hot mixture gradually until the egg yolks are fully incorporated.
5. **Cook the Custard:**
    - Pour the egg yolk mixture back into the saucepan with the remaining milk and cream. Cook the mixture over low heat, stirring constantly, until it thickens enough to coat the back of a spoon. This usually takes about 5-7 minutes.
6. **Add Vanilla Extract:**
    - Remove the custard from the heat and stir in the vanilla extract.
7. **Chill the Custard:**
    - Pour the custard into a clean bowl and cover it with plastic wrap, pressing the plastic wrap directly onto the surface to prevent a skin from forming. Refrigerate the custard for at least 4 hours, or overnight, until it is thoroughly chilled.
8. **Churn the Ice Cream:**

- Once the custard is chilled, pour it into an ice cream maker and churn according to the manufacturer's instructions until it reaches a soft-serve consistency.
9. **Freeze the Ice Cream:**
   - Transfer the churned ice cream to an airtight container and freeze for at least 2 hours, or until it is firm enough to scoop.
10. **Serve:**
    - Scoop the mastiha ice cream into bowls or cones and enjoy this unique Greek treat!

Greek Yogurt Ice Cream with Honey and Nuts

Ingredients:

- 2 cups Greek yogurt
- 1 cup heavy cream
- 3/4 cup honey
- 1/2 cup sugar
- 1 teaspoon vanilla extract
- 1/2 cup mixed nuts (such as walnuts, almonds, and pistachios), chopped
- 1/4 teaspoon salt

Instructions:

1. **Mix the Yogurt and Honey:**
    - In a large mixing bowl, combine the Greek yogurt and honey. Whisk until smooth and well blended.
2. **Heat the Cream and Sugar:**
    - In a medium saucepan, combine the heavy cream, sugar, and salt. Heat over medium heat, stirring frequently, until the sugar is completely dissolved and the mixture is hot but not boiling.
3. **Combine the Mixtures:**
    - Gradually add the hot cream mixture to the yogurt and honey mixture, whisking constantly until fully combined. Stir in the vanilla extract.
4. **Chill the Mixture:**
    - Cover the bowl with plastic wrap and refrigerate for at least 4 hours, or overnight, until the mixture is thoroughly chilled.
5. **Churn the Ice Cream:**
    - Pour the chilled mixture into an ice cream maker and churn according to the manufacturer's instructions until it reaches a soft-serve consistency.
6. **Add the Nuts:**
    - During the last few minutes of churning, add the chopped nuts to the ice cream maker, allowing them to mix evenly throughout the ice cream.
7. **Freeze the Ice Cream:**
    - Transfer the churned ice cream to an airtight container and freeze for at least 2 hours, or until it is firm enough to scoop.
8. **Serve:**
    - Scoop the Greek yogurt ice cream with honey and nuts into bowls or cones. Enjoy this creamy, nutty treat with a touch of natural sweetness from the honey!

Kaimaki Ice Cream

Ingredients:

- 2 cups whole milk
- 1 cup heavy cream
- 3/4 cup sugar
- 1 tablespoon salep (ground orchid root)
- 1 teaspoon mastiha (mastic) resin, ground into a powder
- 1 teaspoon vanilla extract
- 1/2 teaspoon ground mastic gum

Instructions:

1. **Prepare the Salep and Mastiha:**
    - In a small bowl, mix the salep and ground mastiha with 1/4 cup of the sugar. This helps prevent clumping when added to the milk.
2. **Heat the Milk and Cream:**
    - In a medium saucepan, combine the whole milk and heavy cream. Heat over medium heat until it begins to steam, but do not let it boil.
3. **Add the Salep Mixture:**
    - Gradually whisk the salep mixture into the hot milk and cream. Continue to whisk until the mixture is smooth and free of lumps.
4. **Add the Remaining Sugar:**
    - Add the remaining sugar to the saucepan, stirring until it is completely dissolved.
5. **Cook the Custard:**
    - Continue to cook the mixture over low heat, stirring constantly, until it thickens enough to coat the back of a spoon. This usually takes about 10-12 minutes.
6. **Add the Vanilla Extract:**
    - Remove the custard from the heat and stir in the vanilla extract.
7. **Chill the Custard:**
    - Pour the custard into a clean bowl and cover it with plastic wrap, pressing the plastic wrap directly onto the surface to prevent a skin from forming. Refrigerate the custard for at least 4 hours, or overnight, until it is thoroughly chilled.
8. **Churn the Ice Cream:**

- Once the custard is chilled, pour it into an ice cream maker and churn according to the manufacturer's instructions until it reaches a soft-serve consistency.
9. **Freeze the Ice Cream:**
   - Transfer the churned ice cream to an airtight container and freeze for at least 2 hours, or until it is firm enough to scoop.
10. **Serve:**
    - Scoop the kaimaki ice cream into bowls or cones and enjoy this traditional Greek dessert with its unique chewy texture and distinct flavor!

Baklava Ice Cream

Ingredients:

For the Ice Cream Base:

- 2 cups whole milk
- 1 cup heavy cream
- 3/4 cup sugar
- 4 egg yolks
- 1 teaspoon vanilla extract
- 1/2 teaspoon ground cinnamon

For the Baklava Mix-In:

- 1 cup chopped mixed nuts (such as walnuts, almonds, and pistachios)
- 1/4 cup honey
- 1 teaspoon ground cinnamon
- 1/4 teaspoon ground cloves
- 1/4 teaspoon ground nutmeg
- 1/4 cup finely chopped phyllo pastry, baked until crispy

Instructions:

1. **Prepare the Ice Cream Base:**
    - **Heat the Milk and Cream:**
        - In a medium saucepan, combine the whole milk and heavy cream. Heat over medium heat until it begins to steam, but do not let it boil.
    - **Whisk the Egg Yolks:**
        - In a separate bowl, whisk the egg yolks with the sugar until they become thick and pale.
    - **Temper the Egg Yolks:**
        - Gradually add a small amount of the hot milk and cream mixture to the egg yolks, whisking constantly to prevent curdling. Continue adding the hot mixture gradually until the egg yolks are fully incorporated.
    - **Cook the Custard:**
        - Pour the egg yolk mixture back into the saucepan with the remaining milk and cream. Cook over low heat, stirring constantly, until the custard thickens enough to coat the back of a spoon (about 5-7 minutes).

- **Add Vanilla and Cinnamon:**
    - Remove the custard from the heat and stir in the vanilla extract and ground cinnamon.
- **Chill the Custard:**
    - Pour the custard into a clean bowl and cover it with plastic wrap, pressing the plastic wrap directly onto the surface to prevent a skin from forming. Refrigerate the custard for at least 4 hours, or overnight, until thoroughly chilled.

2. **Prepare the Baklava Mix-In:**
   - **Mix the Nuts and Spices:**
     - In a bowl, combine the chopped mixed nuts, honey, ground cinnamon, ground cloves, and ground nutmeg. Stir until the nuts are evenly coated.
   - **Bake the Phyllo:**
     - Preheat the oven to 350°F (175°C). Spread the chopped phyllo pastry on a baking sheet and bake until crispy, about 5-7 minutes. Allow it to cool.

3. **Churn the Ice Cream:**
   - **Churn the Custard:**
     - Pour the chilled custard into an ice cream maker and churn according to the manufacturer's instructions until it reaches a soft-serve consistency.
   - **Add the Baklava Mix-In:**
     - During the last few minutes of churning, add the nut mixture and the crispy phyllo pastry, allowing them to mix evenly throughout the ice cream.

4. **Freeze the Ice Cream:**
   - **Transfer to Container:**
     - Transfer the churned ice cream to an airtight container and freeze for at least 2 hours, or until it is firm enough to scoop.

5. **Serve:**
   - **Scoop and Enjoy:**
     - Scoop the baklava ice cream into bowls or cones. Enjoy the rich, nutty flavors and the delightful texture of this baklava-inspired treat!

Ouzo Ice Cream

Ingredients:

- 2 cups whole milk
- 1 cup heavy cream
- 3/4 cup sugar
- 4 egg yolks
- 1/4 cup ouzo
- 1 teaspoon vanilla extract
- 1/4 teaspoon salt
- 1/2 teaspoon anise extract (optional, for extra anise flavor)

Instructions:

1. **Heat the Milk and Cream:**
    - In a medium saucepan, combine the whole milk and heavy cream. Heat over medium heat until it begins to steam, but do not let it boil.
2. **Whisk the Egg Yolks:**
    - In a separate bowl, whisk the egg yolks with the sugar and salt until the mixture becomes thick and pale.
3. **Temper the Egg Yolks:**
    - Gradually add a small amount of the hot milk and cream mixture to the egg yolks, whisking constantly to prevent the eggs from curdling. Continue adding the hot mixture gradually until the egg yolks are fully incorporated.
4. **Cook the Custard:**
    - Pour the egg yolk mixture back into the saucepan with the remaining milk and cream. Cook over low heat, stirring constantly, until the custard thickens enough to coat the back of a spoon (about 5-7 minutes).
5. **Add Ouzo and Vanilla Extract:**
    - Remove the custard from the heat and stir in the ouzo, vanilla extract, and anise extract (if using).
6. **Chill the Custard:**
    - Pour the custard into a clean bowl and cover it with plastic wrap, pressing the plastic wrap directly onto the surface to prevent a skin from forming. Refrigerate the custard for at least 4 hours, or overnight, until thoroughly chilled.
7. **Churn the Ice Cream:**

- Once the custard is chilled, pour it into an ice cream maker and churn according to the manufacturer's instructions until it reaches a soft-serve consistency.
8. **Freeze the Ice Cream:**
    - Transfer the churned ice cream to an airtight container and freeze for at least 2 hours, or until it is firm enough to scoop.
9. **Serve:**
    - Scoop the ouzo ice cream into bowls or cones. Enjoy the unique, licorice-like flavor of this Greek-inspired treat!

Lemon Basil Sorbet

Ingredients:

- 1 cup fresh basil leaves, packed
- 1 cup water
- 1 cup sugar
- 1 cup freshly squeezed lemon juice (about 4-5 lemons)
- 1 tablespoon lemon zest
- 1/4 cup light corn syrup (optional, for a smoother texture)

Instructions:

1. **Make the Basil Syrup:**
   - In a medium saucepan, combine the water and sugar. Heat over medium heat, stirring occasionally, until the sugar is completely dissolved.
   - Once the sugar is dissolved, remove the saucepan from heat and add the basil leaves. Let the basil steep in the hot syrup for about 15-20 minutes to infuse the flavor.
2. **Blend the Basil Syrup:**
   - After steeping, strain the basil leaves out of the syrup and transfer the syrup to a blender. Add the lemon juice, lemon zest, and light corn syrup (if using). Blend until smooth and well combined.
3. **Chill the Mixture:**
   - Pour the blended mixture into a clean bowl and cover it with plastic wrap. Refrigerate the mixture for at least 2 hours, or until it is thoroughly chilled.
4. **Churn the Sorbet:**
   - Once the mixture is chilled, pour it into an ice cream maker and churn according to the manufacturer's instructions until it reaches a smooth, sorbet-like consistency.
5. **Freeze the Sorbet:**
   - Transfer the churned sorbet to an airtight container and freeze for at least 2 hours, or until it is firm enough to scoop.
6. **Serve:**
   - Scoop the lemon basil sorbet into bowls or cones. Enjoy the refreshing and vibrant flavors of this zesty treat!

This sorbet is perfect for a light, refreshing dessert with a unique twist of basil.

Feta Cheese Ice Cream

Ingredients:

- 2 cups whole milk
- 1 cup heavy cream
- 3/4 cup sugar
- 4 egg yolks
- 1 cup crumbled feta cheese
- 1 teaspoon vanilla extract
- 1/4 teaspoon salt
- Zest of 1 lemon

Instructions:

1. **Heat the Milk and Cream:**
    - In a medium saucepan, combine the whole milk and heavy cream. Heat over medium heat until it begins to steam, but do not let it boil.
2. **Whisk the Egg Yolks:**
    - In a separate bowl, whisk the egg yolks with the sugar and salt until the mixture becomes thick and pale.
3. **Temper the Egg Yolks:**
    - Gradually add a small amount of the hot milk and cream mixture to the egg yolks, whisking constantly to prevent the eggs from curdling. Continue adding the hot mixture gradually until the egg yolks are fully incorporated.
4. **Cook the Custard:**
    - Pour the egg yolk mixture back into the saucepan with the remaining milk and cream. Cook over low heat, stirring constantly, until the custard thickens enough to coat the back of a spoon (about 5-7 minutes).
5. **Add the Feta Cheese:**
    - Remove the custard from the heat and stir in the crumbled feta cheese. Use an immersion blender or transfer the mixture to a regular blender to blend until smooth.
6. **Add Vanilla Extract and Lemon Zest:**
    - Stir in the vanilla extract and lemon zest.
7. **Chill the Custard:**
    - Pour the custard into a clean bowl and cover it with plastic wrap, pressing the plastic wrap directly onto the surface to prevent a skin from forming. Refrigerate the custard for at least 4 hours, or overnight, until thoroughly chilled.

8. **Churn the Ice Cream:**
    - Once the custard is chilled, pour it into an ice cream maker and churn according to the manufacturer's instructions until it reaches a soft-serve consistency.
9. **Freeze the Ice Cream:**
    - Transfer the churned ice cream to an airtight container and freeze for at least 2 hours, or until it is firm enough to scoop.
10. **Serve:**
    - Scoop the feta cheese ice cream into bowls or cones. Enjoy the creamy, tangy flavor of this unique dessert!

This ice cream pairs well with fresh fruit, such as figs or strawberries, and can also be served with a drizzle of honey for added sweetness.

Halva Ice Cream

Ingredients:

- 2 cups whole milk
- 1 cup heavy cream
- 3/4 cup sugar
- 4 egg yolks
- 1 cup crumbled halva (plain or flavored)
- 1 teaspoon vanilla extract
- 1/4 teaspoon salt

Instructions:

1. **Heat the Milk and Cream:**
    - In a medium saucepan, combine the whole milk and heavy cream. Heat over medium heat until it begins to steam, but do not let it boil.
2. **Whisk the Egg Yolks:**
    - In a separate bowl, whisk the egg yolks with the sugar and salt until the mixture becomes thick and pale.
3. **Temper the Egg Yolks:**
    - Gradually add a small amount of the hot milk and cream mixture to the egg yolks, whisking constantly to prevent the eggs from curdling. Continue adding the hot mixture gradually until the egg yolks are fully incorporated.
4. **Cook the Custard:**
    - Pour the egg yolk mixture back into the saucepan with the remaining milk and cream. Cook over low heat, stirring constantly, until the custard thickens enough to coat the back of a spoon (about 5-7 minutes).
5. **Add the Halva:**
    - Remove the custard from the heat and stir in the crumbled halva. Stir until the halva is mostly dissolved into the custard, leaving some small chunks for texture.
6. **Add Vanilla Extract:**
    - Stir in the vanilla extract.
7. **Chill the Custard:**
    - Pour the custard into a clean bowl and cover it with plastic wrap, pressing the plastic wrap directly onto the surface to prevent a skin from forming. Refrigerate the custard for at least 4 hours, or overnight, until thoroughly chilled.
8. **Churn the Ice Cream:**

- Once the custard is chilled, pour it into an ice cream maker and churn according to the manufacturer's instructions until it reaches a soft-serve consistency.

9. **Freeze the Ice Cream:**
    - Transfer the churned ice cream to an airtight container and freeze for at least 2 hours, or until it is firm enough to scoop.
10. **Serve:**
    - Scoop the halva ice cream into bowls or cones. Enjoy the rich, nutty flavor and unique texture of this Mediterranean-inspired dessert!

This ice cream is delightful on its own or served with a drizzle of honey or a sprinkle of toasted sesame seeds for added flavor and texture.

Loukoumi Ice Cream

Ingredients:

- 2 cups whole milk
- 1 cup heavy cream
- 3/4 cup sugar
- 4 egg yolks
- 1/2 cup loukoumi (Greek Turkish delight), chopped into small pieces
- 1 teaspoon vanilla extract
- 1/4 teaspoon salt
- Optional: 1 tablespoon rosewater or orange blossom water for added flavor

Instructions:

1. **Heat the Milk and Cream:**
    - In a medium saucepan, combine the whole milk and heavy cream. Heat over medium heat until it begins to steam, but do not let it boil.
2. **Whisk the Egg Yolks:**
    - In a separate bowl, whisk the egg yolks with the sugar and salt until the mixture becomes thick and pale.
3. **Temper the Egg Yolks:**
    - Gradually add a small amount of the hot milk and cream mixture to the egg yolks, whisking constantly to prevent the eggs from curdling. Continue adding the hot mixture gradually until the egg yolks are fully incorporated.
4. **Cook the Custard:**
    - Pour the egg yolk mixture back into the saucepan with the remaining milk and cream. Cook over low heat, stirring constantly, until the custard thickens enough to coat the back of a spoon (about 5-7 minutes).
5. **Add the Loukoumi:**
    - Remove the custard from the heat and stir in the chopped loukoumi pieces. Stir until the loukoumi begins to melt into the custard.
6. **Add Vanilla Extract (and optional flavoring):**
    - Stir in the vanilla extract. If using rosewater or orange blossom water, add it at this stage for additional flavor.
7. **Chill the Custard:**
    - Pour the custard into a clean bowl and cover it with plastic wrap, pressing the plastic wrap directly onto the surface to prevent a skin from forming. Refrigerate the custard for at least 4 hours, or overnight, until thoroughly chilled.

8. **Churn the Ice Cream:**
   - Once the custard is chilled, pour it into an ice cream maker and churn according to the manufacturer's instructions until it reaches a soft-serve consistency.
9. **Freeze the Ice Cream:**
   - Transfer the churned ice cream to an airtight container and freeze for at least 2 hours, or until it is firm enough to scoop.
10. **Serve:**
    - Scoop the loukoumi ice cream into bowls or cones. Enjoy the delightful blend of creamy custard with the chewy, sweet pieces of loukoumi!

This ice cream captures the essence of loukoumi, a traditional Greek and Turkish treat, and is perfect for a refreshing dessert with a unique texture and flavor profile.

Metaxa Ice Cream

Ingredients:

- 2 cups whole milk
- 1 cup heavy cream
- 3/4 cup sugar
- 4 egg yolks
- 1/2 cup Metaxa brandy
- 1 teaspoon vanilla extract
- 1/4 teaspoon salt

Instructions:

1. **Heat the Milk and Cream:**
    - In a medium saucepan, combine the whole milk and heavy cream. Heat over medium heat until it begins to steam, but do not let it boil.
2. **Whisk the Egg Yolks:**
    - In a separate bowl, whisk the egg yolks with the sugar and salt until the mixture becomes thick and pale.
3. **Temper the Egg Yolks:**
    - Gradually add a small amount of the hot milk and cream mixture to the egg yolks, whisking constantly to prevent the eggs from curdling. Continue adding the hot mixture gradually until the egg yolks are fully incorporated.
4. **Cook the Custard:**
    - Pour the egg yolk mixture back into the saucepan with the remaining milk and cream. Cook over low heat, stirring constantly, until the custard thickens enough to coat the back of a spoon (about 5-7 minutes).
5. **Add the Metaxa Brandy:**
    - Remove the custard from the heat and stir in the Metaxa brandy. Stir well to combine.
6. **Add Vanilla Extract:**
    - Stir in the vanilla extract.
7. **Chill the Custard:**
    - Pour the custard into a clean bowl and cover it with plastic wrap, pressing the plastic wrap directly onto the surface to prevent a skin from forming. Refrigerate the custard for at least 4 hours, or overnight, until thoroughly chilled.
8. **Churn the Ice Cream:**

- Once the custard is chilled, pour it into an ice cream maker and churn according to the manufacturer's instructions until it reaches a soft-serve consistency.
9. **Freeze the Ice Cream:**
    - Transfer the churned ice cream to an airtight container and freeze for at least 2 hours, or until it is firm enough to scoop.
10. **Serve:**
    - Scoop the Metaxa ice cream into bowls or cones. Enjoy the rich, smooth flavor of this Greek brandy-infused dessert!

This ice cream is perfect for adults looking to enjoy the unique taste of Metaxa in a refreshing and creamy treat. Adjust the amount of brandy according to your preference for a stronger or milder flavor.

Orange Blossom Ice Cream

Ingredients:

- 2 cups whole milk
- 1 cup heavy cream
- 3/4 cup sugar
- 4 egg yolks
- 1 tablespoon orange blossom water
- Zest of 2 oranges
- 1 teaspoon vanilla extract
- 1/4 teaspoon salt

Instructions:

1. **Heat the Milk and Cream:**
   - In a medium saucepan, combine the whole milk and heavy cream. Heat over medium heat until it begins to steam, but do not let it boil.
2. **Whisk the Egg Yolks:**
   - In a separate bowl, whisk the egg yolks with the sugar and salt until the mixture becomes thick and pale.
3. **Temper the Egg Yolks:**
   - Gradually add a small amount of the hot milk and cream mixture to the egg yolks, whisking constantly to prevent the eggs from curdling. Continue adding the hot mixture gradually until the egg yolks are fully incorporated.
4. **Cook the Custard:**
   - Pour the egg yolk mixture back into the saucepan with the remaining milk and cream. Cook over low heat, stirring constantly, until the custard thickens enough to coat the back of a spoon (about 5-7 minutes).
5. **Add Orange Blossom Water and Zest:**
   - Remove the custard from the heat and stir in the orange blossom water and orange zest. Stir well to combine.
6. **Add Vanilla Extract:**
   - Stir in the vanilla extract.
7. **Chill the Custard:**
   - Pour the custard into a clean bowl and cover it with plastic wrap, pressing the plastic wrap directly onto the surface to prevent a skin from forming. Refrigerate the custard for at least 4 hours, or overnight, until thoroughly chilled.
8. **Churn the Ice Cream:**

- Once the custard is chilled, pour it into an ice cream maker and churn according to the manufacturer's instructions until it reaches a soft-serve consistency.

9. **Freeze the Ice Cream:**
   - Transfer the churned ice cream to an airtight container and freeze for at least 2 hours, or until it is firm enough to scoop.
10. **Serve:**
    - Scoop the orange blossom ice cream into bowls or cones. Enjoy the delicate floral flavor and citrusy zest of this refreshing dessert!

This ice cream captures the essence of orange blossom with its floral aroma and pairs beautifully with fresh fruit or as a standalone treat. Adjust the amount of orange blossom water according to your preference for a more subtle or pronounced flavor.

Olive Oil Ice Cream

Ingredients:

- 2 cups whole milk
- 1 cup heavy cream
- 3/4 cup sugar
- 4 egg yolks
- 1/2 cup extra virgin olive oil
- 1 teaspoon vanilla extract
- 1/4 teaspoon salt

Instructions:

1. **Heat the Milk and Cream:**
   - In a medium saucepan, combine the whole milk and heavy cream. Heat over medium heat until it begins to steam, but do not let it boil.
2. **Whisk the Egg Yolks:**
   - In a separate bowl, whisk the egg yolks with the sugar and salt until the mixture becomes thick and pale.
3. **Temper the Egg Yolks:**
   - Gradually add a small amount of the hot milk and cream mixture to the egg yolks, whisking constantly to prevent the eggs from curdling. Continue adding the hot mixture gradually until the egg yolks are fully incorporated.
4. **Cook the Custard:**
   - Pour the egg yolk mixture back into the saucepan with the remaining milk and cream. Cook over low heat, stirring constantly, until the custard thickens enough to coat the back of a spoon (about 5-7 minutes).
5. **Add the Olive Oil:**
   - Remove the custard from the heat and slowly whisk in the extra virgin olive oil. Whisk until the olive oil is fully incorporated and the mixture is smooth.
6. **Add Vanilla Extract:**
   - Stir in the vanilla extract.
7. **Chill the Custard:**
   - Pour the custard into a clean bowl and cover it with plastic wrap, pressing the plastic wrap directly onto the surface to prevent a skin from forming. Refrigerate the custard for at least 4 hours, or overnight, until thoroughly chilled.
8. **Churn the Ice Cream:**

- Once the custard is chilled, pour it into an ice cream maker and churn according to the manufacturer's instructions until it reaches a soft-serve consistency.
9. **Freeze the Ice Cream:**
    - Transfer the churned ice cream to an airtight container and freeze for at least 2 hours, or until it is firm enough to scoop.
10. **Serve:**
    - Scoop the olive oil ice cream into bowls or cones. Enjoy the smooth, creamy texture and the subtle, savory notes of extra virgin olive oil in this unique dessert!

This ice cream is a delightful blend of sweet and savory flavors, perfect for those who appreciate the Mediterranean taste of olive oil. Adjust the amount of olive oil according to your preference for a more pronounced or milder flavor.

Pistachio Ice Cream

Ingredients:

- 2 cups whole milk
- 1 cup heavy cream
- 3/4 cup sugar
- 4 egg yolks
- 1 cup shelled pistachios, unsalted
- 1 teaspoon vanilla extract
- 1/4 teaspoon almond extract (optional, for enhanced nuttiness)
- 1/4 teaspoon salt

Instructions:

1. **Prepare the Pistachios:**
   - In a food processor or blender, pulse the pistachios until finely ground but not turned into a paste. Set aside.
2. **Heat the Milk and Cream:**
   - In a medium saucepan, combine the whole milk and heavy cream. Heat over medium heat until it begins to steam, but do not let it boil.
3. **Whisk the Egg Yolks:**
   - In a separate bowl, whisk the egg yolks with the sugar and salt until the mixture becomes thick and pale.
4. **Temper the Egg Yolks:**
   - Gradually add a small amount of the hot milk and cream mixture to the egg yolks, whisking constantly to prevent the eggs from curdling. Continue adding the hot mixture gradually until the egg yolks are fully incorporated.
5. **Cook the Custard:**
   - Pour the egg yolk mixture back into the saucepan with the remaining milk and cream. Cook over low heat, stirring constantly, until the custard thickens enough to coat the back of a spoon (about 5-7 minutes).
6. **Add the Pistachios:**
   - Remove the custard from the heat and stir in the ground pistachios. Mix well until the pistachios are evenly distributed throughout the custard.
7. **Add Vanilla and Almond Extract (if using):**
   - Stir in the vanilla extract and almond extract (if using). These extracts enhance the nutty flavor of the pistachios.
8. **Chill the Custard:**

- Pour the custard into a clean bowl and cover it with plastic wrap, pressing the plastic wrap directly onto the surface to prevent a skin from forming. Refrigerate the custard for at least 4 hours, or overnight, until thoroughly chilled.

9. **Churn the Ice Cream:**
    - Once the custard is chilled, pour it into an ice cream maker and churn according to the manufacturer's instructions until it reaches a soft-serve consistency.
10. **Freeze the Ice Cream:**
    - Transfer the churned pistachio ice cream to an airtight container and freeze for at least 2 hours, or until it is firm enough to scoop.
11. **Serve:**
    - Scoop the pistachio ice cream into bowls or cones. Enjoy the creamy texture and rich, nutty flavor of this classic dessert!

This pistachio ice cream is a delightful treat, perfect for enjoying on its own or paired with desserts like baklava or fresh fruit. Adjust the sweetness by varying the amount of sugar according to your taste preferences.

Melomakarona Ice Cream

Ingredients:

- 2 cups whole milk
- 1 cup heavy cream
- 3/4 cup sugar
- 4 egg yolks
- 1/2 cup honey
- 1/2 cup finely chopped walnuts
- Zest of 1 orange
- 1 teaspoon ground cinnamon
- 1/4 teaspoon ground cloves
- 1/4 teaspoon ground nutmeg
- 1 teaspoon vanilla extract
- Pinch of salt

Instructions:

1. **Prepare the Milk and Cream Mixture:**
    - In a medium saucepan, combine the whole milk and heavy cream. Heat over medium heat until it begins to steam, but do not let it boil. Remove from heat and set aside.
2. **Whisk the Egg Yolks:**
    - In a separate bowl, whisk the egg yolks with the sugar and salt until the mixture becomes thick and pale.
3. **Temper the Egg Yolks:**
    - Gradually add a small amount of the hot milk and cream mixture to the egg yolks, whisking constantly to prevent the eggs from curdling. Continue adding the hot mixture gradually until the egg yolks are fully incorporated.
4. **Create the Custard:**
    - Pour the egg yolk mixture back into the saucepan with the remaining milk and cream. Cook over low heat, stirring constantly, until the custard thickens and coats the back of a spoon (about 5-7 minutes).
5. **Add the Honey and Spices:**
    - Remove the custard from heat and stir in the honey, finely chopped walnuts, orange zest, ground cinnamon, ground cloves, and ground nutmeg. Mix well until all ingredients are fully incorporated.
6. **Add Vanilla Extract:**
    - Stir in the vanilla extract to enhance the flavor.

7. **Chill the Custard:**
   - Pour the custard into a clean bowl and cover it with plastic wrap, pressing the plastic wrap directly onto the surface of the custard to prevent a skin from forming. Refrigerate the custard for at least 4 hours or overnight until thoroughly chilled.
8. **Churn the Ice Cream:**
   - Once the custard is chilled, pour it into an ice cream maker and churn according to the manufacturer's instructions until it reaches a soft-serve consistency.
9. **Freeze the Ice Cream:**
   - Transfer the churned Melomakarona ice cream into an airtight container and freeze for at least 2 hours, or until it firms up enough to scoop.
10. **Serve:**
    - Scoop the Melomakarona ice cream into bowls or cones. Enjoy the festive flavors of this Greek dessert in a cool and creamy form!

This ice cream captures the essence of Melomakarona with its honey, spices, and nutty flavors, making it a perfect treat for any occasion, especially during festive seasons. Adjust sweetness and spice levels according to your taste preferences.

Saffron Ice Cream

Ingredients:

- 2 cups whole milk
- 1 cup heavy cream
- 3/4 cup sugar
- 4 egg yolks
- 1/4 teaspoon saffron threads
- 1 tablespoon warm milk (to bloom saffron)
- 1 teaspoon vanilla extract
- Pinch of salt

Instructions:

1. **Prepare Saffron Infusion:**
   - In a small bowl, combine the saffron threads with 1 tablespoon of warm milk. Let it sit for 5-10 minutes to allow the saffron to bloom and release its color and flavor.
2. **Heat the Milk and Cream:**
   - In a medium saucepan, combine the whole milk and heavy cream. Heat over medium heat until it begins to steam, but do not let it boil.
3. **Whisk the Egg Yolks:**
   - In a separate bowl, whisk the egg yolks with the sugar and salt until the mixture becomes thick and pale.
4. **Temper the Egg Yolks:**
   - Gradually add a small amount of the hot milk and cream mixture to the egg yolks, whisking constantly to prevent the eggs from curdling. Continue adding the hot mixture gradually until the egg yolks are fully incorporated.
5. **Add the Saffron Mixture:**
   - Pour the saffron-infused milk into the saucepan with the remaining milk and cream. Stir well to combine.
6. **Cook the Custard:**
   - Cook the custard mixture over low heat, stirring constantly, until it thickens enough to coat the back of a spoon (about 5-7 minutes).
7. **Add Vanilla Extract:**
   - Remove the custard from heat and stir in the vanilla extract.
8. **Chill the Custard:**
   - Pour the custard into a clean bowl and cover it with plastic wrap, pressing the plastic wrap directly onto the surface of the custard to prevent a skin

from forming. Refrigerate the custard for at least 4 hours, or overnight, until thoroughly chilled.

9. **Churn the Ice Cream:**
    - Once the custard is chilled, pour it into an ice cream maker and churn according to the manufacturer's instructions until it reaches a soft-serve consistency.
10. **Freeze the Ice Cream:**
    - Transfer the churned saffron ice cream into an airtight container and freeze for at least 2 hours, or until it firms up enough to scoop.
11. **Serve:**
    - Scoop the saffron ice cream into bowls or cones. Enjoy the delicate floral aroma and subtle flavor of this exotic ice cream!

Saffron ice cream is a luxurious and aromatic treat, perfect for special occasions or for anyone looking to enjoy a unique and sophisticated dessert experience. Adjust the amount of saffron according to your taste preferences for a more pronounced or subtle saffron flavor.

Greek Coffee Ice Cream

Ingredients:

- 2 cups whole milk
- 1 cup heavy cream
- 3/4 cup sugar
- 4 egg yolks
- 3 tablespoons Greek coffee grounds (fine grind)
- 1 teaspoon vanilla extract
- Pinch of salt

Instructions:

1. **Infuse the Milk and Cream:**
   - In a medium saucepan, combine the whole milk and heavy cream. Stir in the Greek coffee grounds. Heat the mixture over medium-low heat until it begins to steam, stirring occasionally. Remove from heat and let it steep for 15-20 minutes to infuse the coffee flavor.
2. **Strain the Mixture:**
   - After steeping, strain the milk and cream mixture through a fine-mesh sieve or cheesecloth to remove the coffee grounds. Press down on the grounds to extract as much flavor as possible. Discard the grounds and return the infused milk and cream to the saucepan.
3. **Prepare the Custard:**
   - In a separate bowl, whisk the egg yolks with the sugar and salt until the mixture becomes thick and pale.
4. **Temper the Egg Yolks:**
   - Gradually add a small amount of the hot infused milk and cream mixture to the egg yolks, whisking constantly to prevent the eggs from curdling. Continue adding the hot mixture gradually until the egg yolks are fully incorporated.
5. **Cook the Custard:**
   - Pour the egg yolk mixture back into the saucepan with the remaining infused milk and cream. Cook over low heat, stirring constantly, until the custard thickens enough to coat the back of a spoon (about 5-7 minutes).
6. **Add Vanilla Extract:**
   - Remove the custard from heat and stir in the vanilla extract.
7. **Chill the Custard:**

- Pour the custard into a clean bowl and cover it with plastic wrap, pressing the plastic wrap directly onto the surface of the custard to prevent a skin from forming. Refrigerate the custard for at least 4 hours, or overnight, until thoroughly chilled.
8. **Churn the Ice Cream:**
    - Once the custard is chilled, pour it into an ice cream maker and churn according to the manufacturer's instructions until it reaches a soft-serve consistency.
9. **Freeze the Ice Cream:**
    - Transfer the churned Greek coffee ice cream into an airtight container and freeze for at least 2 hours, or until it firms up enough to scoop.
10. **Serve:**
    - Scoop the Greek coffee ice cream into bowls or cones. Enjoy the rich, bold flavors of Greek coffee in a cool and creamy dessert!

This ice cream captures the essence of traditional Greek coffee with its strong, aromatic profile, making it a delightful treat for coffee lovers and those who appreciate unique flavors in their desserts. Adjust the sweetness by varying the amount of sugar according to your taste preferences.

Rosewater Ice Cream

Ingredients:

- 2 cups whole milk
- 1 cup heavy cream
- 3/4 cup sugar
- 4 egg yolks
- 1/4 cup rosewater
- 1 teaspoon vanilla extract
- Pinch of salt
- Optional: A few drops of pink food coloring (for a light pink hue)

Instructions:

1. **Prepare the Milk and Cream Mixture:**
   - In a medium saucepan, combine the whole milk and heavy cream. Heat over medium heat until it begins to steam, but do not let it boil.
2. **Whisk the Egg Yolks:**
   - In a separate bowl, whisk the egg yolks with the sugar and salt until the mixture becomes thick and pale.
3. **Temper the Egg Yolks:**
   - Gradually add a small amount of the hot milk and cream mixture to the egg yolks, whisking constantly to prevent the eggs from curdling. Continue adding the hot mixture gradually until the egg yolks are fully incorporated.
4. **Add Rosewater:**
   - Pour the egg yolk mixture back into the saucepan with the remaining milk and cream. Stir in the rosewater.
5. **Cook the Custard:**
   - Cook the custard mixture over low heat, stirring constantly, until it thickens enough to coat the back of a spoon (about 5-7 minutes).
6. **Add Vanilla Extract:**
   - Remove the custard from heat and stir in the vanilla extract.
7. **Optional: Add Food Coloring:**
   - If desired, add a few drops of pink food coloring to achieve a light pink hue.
8. **Chill the Custard:**
   - Pour the custard into a clean bowl and cover it with plastic wrap, pressing the plastic wrap directly onto the surface of the custard to prevent a skin

from forming. Refrigerate the custard for at least 4 hours, or overnight, until thoroughly chilled.

9. **Churn the Ice Cream:**
   - Once the custard is chilled, pour it into an ice cream maker and churn according to the manufacturer's instructions until it reaches a soft-serve consistency.

10. **Freeze the Ice Cream:**
    - Transfer the churned rosewater ice cream into an airtight container and freeze for at least 2 hours, or until it firms up enough to scoop.

11. **Serve:**
    - Scoop the rosewater ice cream into bowls or cones. Enjoy the delicate floral aroma and refreshing taste of this elegant dessert!

This rosewater ice cream is perfect for a special occasion or as a refreshing treat during warmer months. Adjust the amount of rosewater according to your taste preferences for a more subtle or pronounced floral flavor.

Mastic and Almond Ice Cream

Ingredients:

- 2 cups whole milk
- 1 cup heavy cream
- 3/4 cup sugar
- 4 egg yolks
- 1/2 teaspoon mastic gum powder (or finely ground mastic resin)
- 1/2 cup almond flakes or chopped almonds
- 1 teaspoon vanilla extract
- Pinch of salt

Instructions:

1. **Prepare Mastic Infusion:**
   - In a mortar and pestle, grind the mastic gum into a fine powder. Alternatively, use mastic gum powder if available.
2. **Heat the Milk and Cream:**
   - In a medium saucepan, combine the whole milk and heavy cream. Heat over medium heat until it begins to steam, but do not let it boil.
3. **Infuse the Mastic:**
   - Add the ground mastic gum to the milk and cream mixture. Stir well to dissolve the mastic powder. Let it steep over low heat for 10-15 minutes to infuse the flavor. Stir occasionally.
4. **Whisk the Egg Yolks:**
   - In a separate bowl, whisk the egg yolks with the sugar and salt until the mixture becomes thick and pale.
5. **Temper the Egg Yolks:**
   - Gradually add a small amount of the hot milk and cream mixture to the egg yolks, whisking constantly to prevent the eggs from curdling. Continue adding the hot mixture gradually until the egg yolks are fully incorporated.
6. **Create the Custard:**
   - Pour the egg yolk mixture back into the saucepan with the infused milk and cream. Cook over low heat, stirring constantly, until the custard thickens enough to coat the back of a spoon (about 5-7 minutes).
7. **Add Almonds and Vanilla Extract:**
   - Remove the custard from heat and stir in the almond flakes (or chopped almonds) and vanilla extract. Mix well to evenly distribute the almonds.
8. **Chill the Custard:**

- Pour the custard into a clean bowl and cover it with plastic wrap, pressing the plastic wrap directly onto the surface of the custard to prevent a skin from forming. Refrigerate the custard for at least 4 hours, or overnight, until thoroughly chilled.

9. **Churn the Ice Cream:**
    - Once the custard is chilled, pour it into an ice cream maker and churn according to the manufacturer's instructions until it reaches a soft-serve consistency.
10. **Freeze the Ice Cream:**
    - Transfer the churned mastic and almond ice cream into an airtight container and freeze for at least 2 hours, or until it firms up enough to scoop.
11. **Serve:**
    - Scoop the mastic and almond ice cream into bowls or cones. Enjoy the unique blend of mastic's subtle pine and almond's nutty flavors in this Mediterranean-inspired dessert!

This ice cream is a wonderful fusion of flavors, combining the distinctive taste of mastic with the crunchiness of almonds, perfect for those looking to explore new and intriguing dessert options. Adjust sweetness by varying the amount of sugar according to your taste preferences.

Spiced Fig Ice Cream

Ingredients:

- 2 cups whole milk
- 1 cup heavy cream
- 3/4 cup sugar
- 4 egg yolks
- 1 cup fresh figs, chopped (about 6-8 figs)
- 1 teaspoon ground cinnamon
- 1/4 teaspoon ground nutmeg
- 1/4 teaspoon ground cloves
- 1 teaspoon vanilla extract
- Pinch of salt

Instructions:

1. **Prepare the Figs:**
    - Wash and chop the fresh figs into small pieces. Set aside.
2. **Heat the Milk and Cream:**
    - In a medium saucepan, combine the whole milk and heavy cream. Heat over medium heat until it begins to steam, but do not let it boil.
3. **Whisk the Egg Yolks:**
    - In a separate bowl, whisk the egg yolks with the sugar and salt until the mixture becomes thick and pale.
4. **Temper the Egg Yolks:**
    - Gradually add a small amount of the hot milk and cream mixture to the egg yolks, whisking constantly to prevent the eggs from curdling. Continue adding the hot mixture gradually until the egg yolks are fully incorporated.
5. **Cook the Custard:**
    - Pour the egg yolk mixture back into the saucepan with the remaining milk and cream. Cook over low heat, stirring constantly, until the custard thickens enough to coat the back of a spoon (about 5-7 minutes).
6. **Add the Figs and Spices:**
    - Remove the custard from heat and stir in the chopped figs, ground cinnamon, ground nutmeg, and ground cloves. Mix well to combine.
7. **Add Vanilla Extract:**
    - Stir in the vanilla extract.
8. **Chill the Custard:**

- Pour the custard into a clean bowl and cover it with plastic wrap, pressing the plastic wrap directly onto the surface of the custard to prevent a skin from forming. Refrigerate the custard for at least 4 hours, or overnight, until thoroughly chilled.

9. **Churn the Ice Cream:**
    - Once the custard is chilled, pour it into an ice cream maker and churn according to the manufacturer's instructions until it reaches a soft-serve consistency.
10. **Freeze the Ice Cream:**
    - Transfer the churned spiced fig ice cream into an airtight container and freeze for at least 2 hours, or until it firms up enough to scoop.
11. **Serve:**
    - Scoop the spiced fig ice cream into bowls or cones. Enjoy the rich, sweet flavor and warm spices of this unique dessert!

This spiced fig ice cream is perfect for those who enjoy the natural sweetness of figs combined with comforting spices. Adjust the amount of spices and sweetness according to your taste preferences for a more pronounced or subtle flavor profile.

Grapefruit Mint Sorbet

Ingredients:

- 2 cups fresh grapefruit juice (from about 3-4 large grapefruits)
- 1 cup water
- 1 cup sugar
- Zest of 1 grapefruit
- 1/4 cup fresh mint leaves, chopped
- 2 tablespoons fresh lemon juice

Instructions:

1. **Prepare Grapefruit Juice:**
    - Juice the grapefruits to get 2 cups of fresh grapefruit juice. Strain the juice to remove any pulp and seeds. Set aside.
2. **Make Simple Syrup:**
    - In a small saucepan, combine water and sugar. Heat over medium heat, stirring occasionally, until the sugar completely dissolves and the mixture just begins to boil. Remove from heat and let it cool slightly.
3. **Infuse with Mint and Grapefruit Zest:**
    - Stir in the chopped mint leaves and grapefruit zest into the warm simple syrup. Let it steep for about 10-15 minutes to infuse the flavors.
4. **Combine Ingredients:**
    - In a large bowl, combine the infused syrup mixture (strained to remove mint leaves and zest) with the fresh grapefruit juice and lemon juice. Stir well to combine.
5. **Chill the Mixture:**
    - Cover the bowl with plastic wrap and refrigerate the mixture until thoroughly chilled, at least 2-3 hours or overnight.
6. **Churn the Sorbet:**
    - Once the mixture is chilled, pour it into an ice cream maker and churn according to the manufacturer's instructions until it reaches a smooth and slushy consistency.
7. **Freeze the Sorbet:**
    - Transfer the churned grapefruit mint sorbet into an airtight container. Press a piece of parchment paper or plastic wrap directly onto the surface of the sorbet to prevent ice crystals from forming. Freeze for an additional 2-3 hours, or until firm.
8. **Serve:**

- - Scoop the grapefruit mint sorbet into bowls or cones. Garnish with fresh mint leaves or a slice of grapefruit if desired. Enjoy the refreshing and tangy flavors!

This Grapefruit Mint Sorbet is a perfect palate cleanser or a refreshing dessert on a hot day. The combination of citrusy grapefruit and aromatic mint creates a delightful balance of flavors that is both cooling and invigorating. Adjust the sweetness by varying the amount of sugar according to your taste preferences.

Mastelo Cheese Ice Cream

Ingredients:

- 2 cups whole milk
- 1 cup heavy cream
- 3/4 cup sugar
- 4 oz Mastelo cheese, grated or finely crumbled
- 4 egg yolks
- 1 teaspoon vanilla extract
- Pinch of salt

Instructions:

1. **Prepare the Mastelo Cheese:**
    - Grate or finely crumble the Mastelo cheese into small pieces. Set aside.
2. **Heat the Milk and Cream:**
    - In a medium saucepan, combine the whole milk and heavy cream. Heat over medium heat until it begins to steam, but do not let it boil.
3. **Add Mastelo Cheese:**
    - Stir in the grated or crumbled Mastelo cheese into the milk and cream mixture. Continue stirring until the cheese is fully melted and incorporated.
4. **Whisk the Egg Yolks:**
    - In a separate bowl, whisk the egg yolks with the sugar and salt until the mixture becomes thick and pale.
5. **Temper the Egg Yolks:**
    - Gradually add a small amount of the hot milk and cream mixture to the egg yolks, whisking constantly to prevent the eggs from curdling. Continue adding the hot mixture gradually until the egg yolks are fully incorporated.
6. **Create the Custard:**
    - Pour the egg yolk mixture back into the saucepan with the Mastelo cheese-infused milk and cream. Cook over low heat, stirring constantly, until the custard thickens enough to coat the back of a spoon (about 5-7 minutes).
7. **Add Vanilla Extract:**
    - Remove the custard from heat and stir in the vanilla extract.
8. **Chill the Custard:**
    - Pour the custard into a clean bowl and cover it with plastic wrap, pressing the plastic wrap directly onto the surface of the custard to prevent a skin

from forming. Refrigerate the custard for at least 4 hours, or overnight, until thoroughly chilled.
9. **Churn the Ice Cream:**
    - Once the custard is chilled, pour it into an ice cream maker and churn according to the manufacturer's instructions until it reaches a soft-serve consistency.
10. **Freeze the Ice Cream:**
    - Transfer the churned Mastelo cheese ice cream into an airtight container and freeze for at least 2 hours, or until it firms up enough to scoop.
11. **Serve:**
    - Scoop the Mastelo cheese ice cream into bowls or cones. Enjoy the unique and savory flavors of this Mediterranean-inspired dessert!

This Mastelo Cheese Ice Cream offers a savory twist on traditional sweet desserts, making it a unique option for those who enjoy exploring unconventional flavors. Adjust the sweetness and saltiness by varying the amount of sugar and cheese according to your taste preferences.

Cinnamon Walnut Ice Cream

Ingredients:

- 2 cups whole milk
- 1 cup heavy cream
- 3/4 cup sugar
- 4 egg yolks
- 1 teaspoon ground cinnamon
- 1 cup walnuts, chopped
- 1 teaspoon vanilla extract
- Pinch of salt

Instructions:

1. **Toast the Walnuts (optional):**
   - Preheat your oven to 350°F (175°C). Spread the chopped walnuts evenly on a baking sheet and toast them in the oven for about 8-10 minutes, stirring occasionally, until fragrant and lightly golden. Remove from the oven and let them cool.
2. **Prepare the Milk and Cream Mixture:**
   - In a medium saucepan, combine the whole milk and heavy cream. Heat over medium heat until it begins to steam, but do not let it boil.
3. **Whisk the Egg Yolks:**
   - In a separate bowl, whisk the egg yolks with the sugar, ground cinnamon, and salt until the mixture becomes thick and pale.
4. **Temper the Egg Yolks:**
   - Gradually add a small amount of the hot milk and cream mixture to the egg yolks, whisking constantly to prevent the eggs from curdling. Continue adding the hot mixture gradually until the egg yolks are fully incorporated.
5. **Create the Custard:**
   - Pour the egg yolk mixture back into the saucepan with the remaining milk and cream. Cook over low heat, stirring constantly, until the custard thickens enough to coat the back of a spoon (about 5-7 minutes).
6. **Add Vanilla Extract and Walnuts:**
   - Remove the custard from heat and stir in the vanilla extract. Let the mixture cool slightly, then fold in the chopped toasted walnuts.
7. **Chill the Custard:**
   - Pour the custard into a clean bowl and cover it with plastic wrap, pressing the plastic wrap directly onto the surface of the custard to prevent a skin

from forming. Refrigerate the custard for at least 4 hours, or overnight, until thoroughly chilled.

8. **Churn the Ice Cream:**
   - Once the custard is chilled, pour it into an ice cream maker and churn according to the manufacturer's instructions until it reaches a soft-serve consistency.
9. **Freeze the Ice Cream:**
   - Transfer the churned cinnamon walnut ice cream into an airtight container and freeze for at least 2 hours, or until it firms up enough to scoop.
10. **Serve:**
    - Scoop the cinnamon walnut ice cream into bowls or cones. Enjoy the creamy texture and warm, nutty flavors of this comforting dessert!

This Cinnamon Walnut Ice Cream offers a delightful blend of sweet cinnamon and crunchy walnuts, perfect for enjoying as a dessert on its own or as a complement to pies and cakes. Adjust the sweetness and cinnamon intensity according to your taste preferences for a personalized treat.

Vanilla Tahini Ice Cream

Ingredients:

- 2 cups whole milk
- 1 cup heavy cream
- 3/4 cup sugar
- 4 egg yolks
- 1/2 cup tahini (well-stirred)
- 1 tablespoon vanilla extract
- Pinch of salt

Instructions:

1. **Prepare Tahini Mixture:**
   - In a small bowl, stir the tahini well to ensure it's smooth and creamy.
2. **Heat the Milk and Cream:**
   - In a medium saucepan, combine the whole milk and heavy cream. Heat over medium heat until it begins to steam, but do not let it boil.
3. **Whisk the Egg Yolks:**
   - In a separate bowl, whisk the egg yolks with the sugar and salt until the mixture becomes thick and pale.
4. **Temper the Egg Yolks:**
   - Gradually add a small amount of the hot milk and cream mixture to the egg yolks, whisking constantly to prevent the eggs from curdling. Continue adding the hot mixture gradually until the egg yolks are fully incorporated.
5. **Add Tahini:**
   - Pour the egg yolk mixture back into the saucepan with the remaining milk and cream. Add the tahini to the mixture and whisk until smooth and well combined.
6. **Cook the Custard:**
   - Cook the custard mixture over low heat, stirring constantly, until it thickens enough to coat the back of a spoon (about 5-7 minutes).
7. **Add Vanilla Extract:**
   - Remove the custard from heat and stir in the vanilla extract.
8. **Chill the Custard:**
   - Pour the custard into a clean bowl and cover it with plastic wrap, pressing the plastic wrap directly onto the surface of the custard to prevent a skin from forming. Refrigerate the custard for at least 4 hours, or overnight, until thoroughly chilled.

9. **Churn the Ice Cream:**
   - Once the custard is chilled, pour it into an ice cream maker and churn according to the manufacturer's instructions until it reaches a soft-serve consistency.
10. **Freeze the Ice Cream:**
    - Transfer the churned vanilla tahini ice cream into an airtight container and freeze for at least 2 hours, or until it firms up enough to scoop.
11. **Serve:**
    - Scoop the vanilla tahini ice cream into bowls or cones. Enjoy the creamy texture and nutty flavor of this unique and delicious dessert!

This Vanilla Tahini Ice Cream offers a delightful twist on classic vanilla with the addition of tahini, creating a smooth and slightly nutty flavor profile. Adjust the sweetness and tahini amount according to your taste preferences for a personalized treat.

Pomegranate Sorbet

Ingredients:

- 2 cups pomegranate juice (freshly squeezed or store-bought)
- 1/2 cup water
- 3/4 cup sugar
- 1 tablespoon fresh lemon juice
- Optional: Pomegranate arils for garnish

Instructions:

1. **Prepare the Simple Syrup:**
    - In a small saucepan, combine water and sugar. Heat over medium heat, stirring occasionally, until the sugar completely dissolves and the mixture just begins to boil. Remove from heat and let it cool slightly.
2. **Combine Ingredients:**
    - In a large bowl, combine the pomegranate juice, fresh lemon juice, and the cooled simple syrup. Stir well to mix.
3. **Chill the Mixture:**
    - Cover the bowl with plastic wrap and refrigerate the mixture until thoroughly chilled, at least 2-3 hours or overnight.
4. **Churn the Sorbet:**
    - Once the mixture is chilled, pour it into an ice cream maker and churn according to the manufacturer's instructions until it reaches a smooth and slushy consistency.
5. **Freeze the Sorbet:**
    - Transfer the churned pomegranate sorbet into an airtight container. Press a piece of parchment paper or plastic wrap directly onto the surface of the sorbet to prevent ice crystals from forming. Freeze for an additional 2-3 hours, or until firm.
6. **Serve:**
    - Scoop the pomegranate sorbet into bowls or cones. Garnish with fresh pomegranate arils if desired. Enjoy the refreshing and tangy flavors!

This Pomegranate Sorbet is perfect for a light and refreshing dessert, especially during hot weather. The tartness of the pomegranate juice combined with the sweetness of the simple syrup creates a balanced and delightful treat. Adjust the sweetness by varying the amount of sugar according to your taste preferences.

Honey Lavender Ice Cream

Ingredients:

- 2 cups whole milk
- 1 cup heavy cream
- 3/4 cup honey
- 3 tablespoons dried culinary lavender buds (or 4-5 fresh lavender sprigs)
- 4 egg yolks
- 1 teaspoon vanilla extract
- Pinch of salt

Instructions:

1. **Infuse Milk and Cream:**
    - In a medium saucepan, combine the whole milk, heavy cream, honey, and dried lavender buds (or fresh lavender sprigs). Heat over medium heat until it begins to steam, stirring occasionally. Once it starts to steam, reduce the heat to low and let it steep for about 10-15 minutes to infuse the lavender flavor. Stir occasionally.
2. **Strain the Mixture:**
    - After steeping, strain the milk and cream mixture through a fine-mesh sieve or cheesecloth to remove the lavender buds or sprigs. Press gently to extract all the flavors.
3. **Whisk the Egg Yolks:**
    - In a separate bowl, whisk the egg yolks with the salt until the mixture becomes thick and pale.
4. **Temper the Egg Yolks:**
    - Gradually add a small amount of the warm infused milk and cream mixture to the egg yolks, whisking constantly to prevent the eggs from curdling. Continue adding the hot mixture gradually until the egg yolks are fully incorporated.
5. **Create the Custard:**
    - Pour the egg yolk mixture back into the saucepan with the remaining infused milk and cream. Cook over low heat, stirring constantly, until the custard thickens enough to coat the back of a spoon (about 5-7 minutes). Do not let it boil.
6. **Add Vanilla Extract:**
    - Remove the custard from heat and stir in the vanilla extract.
7. **Chill the Custard:**

- Pour the custard into a clean bowl and cover it with plastic wrap, pressing the plastic wrap directly onto the surface of the custard to prevent a skin from forming. Refrigerate the custard for at least 4 hours, or overnight, until thoroughly chilled.
8. **Churn the Ice Cream:**
   - Once the custard is chilled, pour it into an ice cream maker and churn according to the manufacturer's instructions until it reaches a soft-serve consistency.
9. **Freeze the Ice Cream:**
   - Transfer the churned honey lavender ice cream into an airtight container and freeze for at least 2 hours, or until it firms up enough to scoop.
10. **Serve:**
    - Scoop the honey lavender ice cream into bowls or cones. Enjoy the delicate floral aroma and sweet honey flavor of this elegant dessert!

This Honey Lavender Ice Cream is perfect for those who enjoy floral-infused treats. Adjust the amount of honey and lavender according to your taste preferences for a more pronounced or subtle flavor. Garnish with fresh lavender petals or a drizzle of honey for an extra touch of elegance.

Raisin and Cinnamon Ice Cream

Ingredients:

- 2 cups whole milk
- 1 cup heavy cream
- 3/4 cup sugar
- 4 egg yolks
- 1 teaspoon ground cinnamon
- 1/2 cup raisins
- 1 teaspoon vanilla extract
- Pinch of salt

Instructions:

1. **Prepare the Raisins:**
    - Place the raisins in a small bowl and cover them with warm water. Let them soak for about 10-15 minutes to plump up. Drain and set aside.
2. **Heat the Milk and Cream:**
    - In a medium saucepan, combine the whole milk and heavy cream. Heat over medium heat until it begins to steam, but do not let it boil.
3. **Whisk the Egg Yolks:**
    - In a separate bowl, whisk the egg yolks with the sugar, ground cinnamon, and salt until the mixture becomes thick and pale.
4. **Temper the Egg Yolks:**
    - Gradually add a small amount of the hot milk and cream mixture to the egg yolks, whisking constantly to prevent the eggs from curdling. Continue adding the hot mixture gradually until the egg yolks are fully incorporated.
5. **Create the Custard:**
    - Pour the egg yolk mixture back into the saucepan with the remaining milk and cream. Cook over low heat, stirring constantly, until the custard thickens enough to coat the back of a spoon (about 5-7 minutes).
6. **Add Vanilla Extract and Raisins:**
    - Remove the custard from heat and stir in the vanilla extract. Let the mixture cool slightly, then fold in the soaked raisins.
7. **Chill the Custard:**
    - Pour the custard into a clean bowl and cover it with plastic wrap, pressing the plastic wrap directly onto the surface of the custard to prevent a skin from forming. Refrigerate the custard for at least 4 hours, or overnight, until thoroughly chilled.

8. **Churn the Ice Cream:**
   - Once the custard is chilled, pour it into an ice cream maker and churn according to the manufacturer's instructions until it reaches a soft-serve consistency.
9. **Freeze the Ice Cream:**
   - Transfer the churned raisin and cinnamon ice cream into an airtight container and freeze for at least 2 hours, or until it firms up enough to scoop.
10. **Serve:**
    - Scoop the raisin and cinnamon ice cream into bowls or cones. Enjoy the creamy texture and warm, comforting flavors of this delightful dessert!

This Raisin and Cinnamon Ice Cream offers a perfect balance of sweetness from the raisins and warmth from the cinnamon, making it a comforting treat. Adjust the amount of cinnamon and sweetness according to your taste preferences for a personalized flavor profile.

Thyme Honey Ice Cream

Ingredients:

- 2 cups whole milk
- 1 cup heavy cream
- 3/4 cup honey
- 4 sprigs fresh thyme (or 1 tablespoon dried thyme)
- 4 egg yolks
- 1 teaspoon vanilla extract
- Pinch of salt

Instructions:

1. **Infuse Milk and Cream with Thyme:**
   - In a medium saucepan, combine the whole milk, heavy cream, honey, and thyme sprigs (or dried thyme). Heat over medium heat until it begins to steam, stirring occasionally. Once it starts to steam, reduce the heat to low and let it steep for about 10-15 minutes to infuse the thyme flavor. Stir occasionally.
2. **Strain the Mixture:**
   - After steeping, strain the milk and cream mixture through a fine-mesh sieve or cheesecloth to remove the thyme sprigs or leaves. Press gently to extract all the flavors.
3. **Whisk the Egg Yolks:**
   - In a separate bowl, whisk the egg yolks with the salt until the mixture becomes thick and pale.
4. **Temper the Egg Yolks:**
   - Gradually add a small amount of the warm infused milk and cream mixture to the egg yolks, whisking constantly to prevent the eggs from curdling. Continue adding the hot mixture gradually until the egg yolks are fully incorporated.
5. **Create the Custard:**
   - Pour the egg yolk mixture back into the saucepan with the remaining infused milk and cream. Cook over low heat, stirring constantly, until the custard thickens enough to coat the back of a spoon (about 5-7 minutes). Do not let it boil.
6. **Add Vanilla Extract:**
   - Remove the custard from heat and stir in the vanilla extract.
7. **Chill the Custard:**

- Pour the custard into a clean bowl and cover it with plastic wrap, pressing the plastic wrap directly onto the surface of the custard to prevent a skin from forming. Refrigerate the custard for at least 4 hours, or overnight, until thoroughly chilled.

8. **Churn the Ice Cream:**
    - Once the custard is chilled, pour it into an ice cream maker and churn according to the manufacturer's instructions until it reaches a soft-serve consistency.
9. **Freeze the Ice Cream:**
    - Transfer the churned thyme honey ice cream into an airtight container and freeze for at least 2 hours, or until it firms up enough to scoop.
10. **Serve:**
    - Scoop the thyme honey ice cream into bowls or cones. Enjoy the delicate herbal notes and sweet honey flavor of this unique and aromatic dessert!

This Thyme Honey Ice Cream offers a sophisticated flavor profile with the earthy essence of thyme complemented by the sweetness of honey. Adjust the amount of honey and thyme according to your taste preferences for a more pronounced or subtle flavor. Garnish with fresh thyme leaves or a drizzle of honey for an elegant presentation.

Greek Mountain Tea Ice Cream

Ingredients:

- 2 cups whole milk
- 1 cup heavy cream
- 3/4 cup sugar
- 4 tablespoons dried Greek mountain tea (also known as Sideritis tea)
- 4 egg yolks
- 1 teaspoon vanilla extract
- Pinch of salt

Instructions:

1. **Infuse Milk and Cream with Greek Mountain Tea:**
    - In a medium saucepan, combine the whole milk, heavy cream, dried Greek mountain tea. Heat over medium heat until it begins to steam, stirring occasionally. Once it starts to steam, reduce the heat to low and let it steep for about 15-20 minutes to infuse the tea flavor. Stir occasionally.
2. **Strain the Mixture:**
    - After steeping, strain the milk and cream mixture through a fine-mesh sieve or cheesecloth to remove the dried Greek mountain tea. Press gently to extract all the flavors.
3. **Whisk the Egg Yolks:**
    - In a separate bowl, whisk the egg yolks with the sugar and salt until the mixture becomes thick and pale.
4. **Temper the Egg Yolks:**
    - Gradually add a small amount of the warm infused milk and cream mixture to the egg yolks, whisking constantly to prevent the eggs from curdling. Continue adding the hot mixture gradually until the egg yolks are fully incorporated.
5. **Create the Custard:**
    - Pour the egg yolk mixture back into the saucepan with the remaining infused milk and cream. Cook over low heat, stirring constantly, until the custard thickens enough to coat the back of a spoon (about 5-7 minutes). Do not let it boil.
6. **Add Vanilla Extract:**
    - Remove the custard from heat and stir in the vanilla extract.
7. **Chill the Custard:**

- Pour the custard into a clean bowl and cover it with plastic wrap, pressing the plastic wrap directly onto the surface of the custard to prevent a skin from forming. Refrigerate the custard for at least 4 hours, or overnight, until thoroughly chilled.

8. **Churn the Ice Cream:**
    - Once the custard is chilled, pour it into an ice cream maker and churn according to the manufacturer's instructions until it reaches a soft-serve consistency.

9. **Freeze the Ice Cream:**
    - Transfer the churned Greek mountain tea ice cream into an airtight container and freeze for at least 2 hours, or until it firms up enough to scoop.

10. **Serve:**
    - Scoop the Greek mountain tea ice cream into bowls or cones. Enjoy the herbal and slightly floral flavors of this unique and refreshing dessert!

This Greek Mountain Tea Ice Cream offers a distinctive herbal taste with hints of floral notes, making it a refreshing choice for those who enjoy exploring new flavors. Adjust the sweetness according to your taste preferences for a personalized treat. Garnish with a sprinkle of dried Greek mountain tea leaves for an extra touch of authenticity.

Lemon Chamomile Sorbet

Ingredients:

- 2 cups water
- 1 cup sugar
- Zest of 2 lemons
- 1/2 cup fresh lemon juice (about 4-5 lemons)
- 4 tablespoons dried chamomile flowers (or 6-8 chamomile tea bags)

Instructions:

1. **Make the Chamomile Infusion:**
    - In a small saucepan, combine the water, sugar, and dried chamomile flowers (or chamomile tea bags). Bring to a simmer over medium heat, stirring occasionally until the sugar is completely dissolved. Remove from heat, cover, and let the chamomile steep for about 15-20 minutes to infuse its flavor.
2. **Strain the Chamomile Mixture:**
    - Strain the chamomile infusion through a fine-mesh sieve or cheesecloth into a clean bowl to remove the chamomile flowers or tea bags. Press gently to extract all the flavors.
3. **Add Lemon Zest and Juice:**
    - Stir in the lemon zest and fresh lemon juice into the chamomile-infused syrup. Mix well to combine.
4. **Chill the Mixture:**
    - Cover the bowl with plastic wrap and refrigerate the mixture until thoroughly chilled, at least 2-3 hours or overnight.
5. **Churn the Sorbet:**
    - Once chilled, pour the lemon chamomile mixture into an ice cream maker and churn according to the manufacturer's instructions until it reaches a slushy consistency.
6. **Freeze the Sorbet:**
    - Transfer the churned sorbet into an airtight container. Press a piece of parchment paper or plastic wrap directly onto the surface of the sorbet to prevent ice crystals from forming. Freeze for an additional 2-3 hours, or until firm.
7. **Serve:**
    - Scoop the lemon chamomile sorbet into bowls or cones. Enjoy the bright citrusy flavor and delicate floral aroma of this refreshing dessert!

This Lemon Chamomile Sorbet is perfect for hot summer days, offering a soothing and refreshing treat with a blend of citrus and floral notes. Adjust the sweetness by varying the amount of sugar according to your taste preferences. Garnish with a sprig of fresh chamomile flowers or a twist of lemon zest for an elegant presentation.

Plum and Anise Ice Cream

Ingredients:

- 2 cups whole milk
- 1 cup heavy cream
- 3/4 cup sugar
- 4 egg yolks
- 4 ripe plums, pitted and chopped
- 1 tablespoon anise seeds
- 1 teaspoon vanilla extract
- Pinch of salt

Instructions:

1. **Infuse Milk and Cream with Plums and Anise:**
    - In a medium saucepan, combine the whole milk, heavy cream, chopped plums, and anise seeds. Heat over medium heat until it begins to steam, stirring occasionally. Once it starts to steam, reduce the heat to low and let it simmer gently for about 15-20 minutes to infuse the flavors. Stir occasionally.
2. **Strain the Mixture:**
    - After simmering, strain the milk and cream mixture through a fine-mesh sieve or cheesecloth to remove the plums and anise seeds. Press gently to extract all the flavors.
3. **Whisk the Egg Yolks:**
    - In a separate bowl, whisk the egg yolks with the sugar and salt until the mixture becomes thick and pale.
4. **Temper the Egg Yolks:**
    - Gradually add a small amount of the warm infused milk and cream mixture to the egg yolks, whisking constantly to prevent the eggs from curdling. Continue adding the hot mixture gradually until the egg yolks are fully incorporated.
5. **Create the Custard:**
    - Pour the egg yolk mixture back into the saucepan with the remaining infused milk and cream. Cook over low heat, stirring constantly, until the custard thickens enough to coat the back of a spoon (about 5-7 minutes). Do not let it boil.
6. **Add Vanilla Extract:**
    - Remove the custard from heat and stir in the vanilla extract.

7. **Chill the Custard:**
   - Pour the custard into a clean bowl and cover it with plastic wrap, pressing the plastic wrap directly onto the surface of the custard to prevent a skin from forming. Refrigerate the custard for at least 4 hours, or overnight, until thoroughly chilled.
8. **Churn the Ice Cream:**
   - Once the custard is chilled, pour it into an ice cream maker and churn according to the manufacturer's instructions until it reaches a soft-serve consistency.
9. **Freeze the Ice Cream:**
   - Transfer the churned plum and anise ice cream into an airtight container and freeze for at least 2 hours, or until it firms up enough to scoop.
10. **Serve:**
    - Scoop the plum and anise ice cream into bowls or cones. Enjoy the sweet, fruity flavor with hints of licorice from the anise seeds in this delightful frozen dessert!

This Plum and Anise Ice Cream offers a delicious blend of sweet plums and aromatic anise, creating a unique and flavorful treat. Adjust the sweetness by varying the amount of sugar according to your taste preferences. Garnish with fresh plum slices or a sprinkle of crushed anise seeds for an extra burst of flavor.

Grape and Ouzo Sorbet

Ingredients:

- 4 cups seedless grapes (green or red), washed and stemmed
- 1/2 cup water
- 1/2 cup sugar
- 1/4 cup ouzo (Greek anise-flavored liqueur)
- Juice of 1 lemon

Instructions:

1. **Prepare the Simple Syrup:**
   - In a small saucepan, combine the water and sugar. Heat over medium heat, stirring occasionally, until the sugar is completely dissolved. Remove from heat and let it cool.
2. **Blend the Grapes:**
   - In a blender or food processor, puree the grapes until smooth.
3. **Strain the Grape Puree:**
   - Strain the grape puree through a fine-mesh sieve or cheesecloth into a clean bowl to remove the seeds and pulp. Press gently to extract as much juice as possible.
4. **Mix the Sorbet Base:**
   - Stir the cooled simple syrup, ouzo, and lemon juice into the strained grape juice. Mix well to combine.
5. **Chill the Mixture:**
   - Cover the bowl with plastic wrap and refrigerate the mixture until thoroughly chilled, at least 2-3 hours or overnight.
6. **Churn the Sorbet:**
   - Once chilled, pour the grape and ouzo mixture into an ice cream maker and churn according to the manufacturer's instructions until it reaches a slushy consistency.
7. **Freeze the Sorbet:**
   - Transfer the churned sorbet into an airtight container. Press a piece of parchment paper or plastic wrap directly onto the surface of the sorbet to prevent ice crystals from forming. Freeze for an additional 2-3 hours, or until firm.
8. **Serve:**

- Scoop the grape and ouzo sorbet into bowls or cones. Enjoy the sweet, fruity flavor with a hint of anise from the ouzo in this refreshing and exotic frozen dessert!

This Grape and Ouzo Sorbet offers a unique combination of flavors that is both sweet and slightly aromatic, making it a perfect treat for a hot summer day. Adjust the sweetness by varying the amount of sugar according to the sweetness of your grapes and your personal taste preferences. Garnish with a sprig of fresh mint or a slice of grape for an extra touch of elegance.

Honey Baklava Ice Cream

Ingredients:

- 2 cups heavy cream
- 1 cup whole milk
- 3/4 cup sugar
- 4 egg yolks
- 1/4 teaspoon salt
- 1/2 cup honey
- 1/2 cup chopped baklava pieces (store-bought or homemade)
- 1 teaspoon vanilla extract
- 1/2 cup chopped walnuts or pistachios (optional, for additional texture)

Instructions:

1. **Prepare the Custard:**
   - In a medium saucepan, combine the heavy cream, whole milk, sugar, and salt. Heat over medium heat, stirring occasionally, until the mixture begins to steam. Do not let it boil.
2. **Whisk the Egg Yolks:**
   - In a separate bowl, whisk the egg yolks until smooth.
3. **Temper the Eggs:**
   - Gradually pour about 1 cup of the hot cream mixture into the egg yolks, whisking constantly to temper the eggs. Gradually add the tempered egg mixture back into the saucepan with the remaining cream mixture, stirring constantly.
4. **Cook the Custard:**
   - Cook the custard over medium-low heat, stirring constantly, until it thickens and coats the back of a spoon, about 8-10 minutes. Remove from heat.
5. **Add Honey and Flavorings:**
   - Stir in the honey and vanilla extract until well combined.
6. **Cool the Custard:**
   - Pour the custard through a fine-mesh sieve into a clean bowl to remove any lumps. Let it cool to room temperature, then cover with plastic wrap, pressing it directly onto the surface of the custard to prevent a skin from forming. Chill in the refrigerator for at least 4 hours or overnight until thoroughly chilled.
7. **Churn the Ice Cream:**

- Once chilled, churn the custard in an ice cream maker according to the manufacturer's instructions until it reaches a soft-serve consistency.
8. **Add Baklava Pieces and Nuts:**
   - During the last few minutes of churning, add the chopped baklava pieces and chopped nuts (if using). Churn until evenly distributed.
9. **Freeze the Ice Cream:**
   - Transfer the churned ice cream into an airtight container, layering with additional baklava pieces and nuts if desired. Press a piece of parchment paper or plastic wrap directly onto the surface of the ice cream to prevent ice crystals from forming. Freeze for at least 4 hours or until firm.
10. **Serve:**
    - Scoop the Honey Baklava Ice Cream into bowls or cones. Garnish with a drizzle of honey or additional chopped nuts if desired. Enjoy the delicious flavors reminiscent of baklava in this creamy, homemade ice cream!

This Honey Baklava Ice Cream is a delightful fusion of creamy ice cream and the rich, nutty flavors of baklava. Adjust the sweetness by varying the amount of honey according to your taste preferences. Serve it as a special dessert for a Mediterranean-inspired treat that is sure to impress!

Cherry Mastelo Ice Cream

Ingredients:

- 2 cups heavy cream
- 1 cup whole milk
- 3/4 cup sugar
- 4 egg yolks
- Pinch of salt
- 1 teaspoon vanilla extract
- 1 cup pitted cherries, chopped
- 1/2 cup crumbled mastelo cheese (or any mild, salty cheese)

Instructions:

1. **Prepare the Custard:**
    - In a medium saucepan, combine the heavy cream, whole milk, sugar, and salt. Heat over medium heat, stirring occasionally, until the mixture begins to steam. Do not let it boil.
2. **Whisk the Egg Yolks:**
    - In a separate bowl, whisk the egg yolks until smooth.
3. **Temper the Eggs:**
    - Gradually pour about 1 cup of the hot cream mixture into the egg yolks, whisking constantly to temper the eggs. Gradually add the tempered egg mixture back into the saucepan with the remaining cream mixture, stirring constantly.
4. **Cook the Custard:**
    - Cook the custard over medium-low heat, stirring constantly, until it thickens and coats the back of a spoon, about 8-10 minutes. Remove from heat.
5. **Add Vanilla Extract:**
    - Stir in the vanilla extract until well combined.
6. **Cool the Custard:**
    - Pour the custard through a fine-mesh sieve into a clean bowl to remove any lumps. Let it cool to room temperature, then cover with plastic wrap, pressing it directly onto the surface of the custard to prevent a skin from forming. Chill in the refrigerator for at least 4 hours or overnight until thoroughly chilled.
7. **Churn the Ice Cream:**

- Once chilled, churn the custard in an ice cream maker according to the manufacturer's instructions until it reaches a soft-serve consistency.
8. **Add Cherries and Mastelo Cheese:**
   - During the last few minutes of churning, add the chopped cherries and crumbled mastelo cheese. Churn until evenly distributed.
9. **Freeze the Ice Cream:**
   - Transfer the churned ice cream into an airtight container, layering with additional cherries and mastelo cheese if desired. Press a piece of parchment paper or plastic wrap directly onto the surface of the ice cream to prevent ice crystals from forming. Freeze for at least 4 hours or until firm.
10. **Serve:**
    - Scoop the Cherry Mastelo Ice Cream into bowls or cones. Garnish with a fresh cherry or a sprinkle of crumbled mastelo cheese. Enjoy the unique combination of sweet cherries and salty cheese in this creamy, homemade ice cream!

This Cherry Mastelo Ice Cream offers a creative twist on traditional flavors, combining the sweetness of cherries with the savory notes of mastelo cheese. Adjust the sweetness by varying the amount of sugar according to your taste preferences. Serve it as a delightful dessert that will intrigue and satisfy your guests!

Pistachio and Mastiha Ice Cream

Ingredients:

- 2 cups heavy cream
- 1 cup whole milk
- 3/4 cup sugar
- 4 egg yolks
- Pinch of salt
- 1 teaspoon vanilla extract
- 1/2 cup shelled pistachios, chopped
- 1 tablespoon mastiha liqueur (mastic liqueur)

Instructions:

1. **Prepare the Custard:**
    - In a medium saucepan, combine the heavy cream, whole milk, sugar, and salt. Heat over medium heat, stirring occasionally, until the mixture begins to steam. Do not let it boil.
2. **Whisk the Egg Yolks:**
    - In a separate bowl, whisk the egg yolks until smooth.
3. **Temper the Eggs:**
    - Gradually pour about 1 cup of the hot cream mixture into the egg yolks, whisking constantly to temper the eggs. Gradually add the tempered egg mixture back into the saucepan with the remaining cream mixture, stirring constantly.
4. **Cook the Custard:**
    - Cook the custard over medium-low heat, stirring constantly, until it thickens and coats the back of a spoon, about 8-10 minutes. Remove from heat.
5. **Add Vanilla Extract and Mastiha Liqueur:**
    - Stir in the vanilla extract and mastiha liqueur until well combined.
6. **Cool the Custard:**
    - Pour the custard through a fine-mesh sieve into a clean bowl to remove any lumps. Let it cool to room temperature, then cover with plastic wrap, pressing it directly onto the surface of the custard to prevent a skin from forming. Chill in the refrigerator for at least 4 hours or overnight until thoroughly chilled.
7. **Toast and Chop Pistachios:**

- While the custard is chilling, toast the chopped pistachios in a dry skillet over medium heat until lightly golden and fragrant. Let them cool completely.
8. **Churn the Ice Cream:**
    - Once chilled, churn the custard in an ice cream maker according to the manufacturer's instructions until it reaches a soft-serve consistency.
9. **Add Pistachios:**
    - During the last few minutes of churning, add the toasted chopped pistachios. Churn until evenly distributed.
10. **Freeze the Ice Cream:**
    - Transfer the churned ice cream into an airtight container, layering with additional chopped pistachios if desired. Press a piece of parchment paper or plastic wrap directly onto the surface of the ice cream to prevent ice crystals from forming. Freeze for at least 4 hours or until firm.
11. **Serve:**
    - Scoop the Pistachio and Mastiha Ice Cream into bowls or cones. Enjoy the creamy texture and distinctive flavors of this unique frozen dessert!

This Pistachio and Mastiha Ice Cream offers a delightful combination of nutty pistachios and the aromatic, resinous flavor of mastiha liqueur. Adjust the sweetness by varying the amount of sugar according to your taste preferences. Serve it as a special treat that will surprise and delight your guests with its exotic flavors!

Greek Yogurt and Figs Ice Cream

Ingredients:

- 2 cups plain Greek yogurt
- 1 cup whole milk
- 3/4 cup sugar
- 4 egg yolks
- Pinch of salt
- 1 teaspoon vanilla extract
- 1 cup fresh figs, chopped (about 8-10 figs)
- 1 tablespoon honey (optional, for added sweetness)

Instructions:

1. **Prepare the Custard:**
    - In a medium saucepan, combine the Greek yogurt, whole milk, sugar, and salt. Heat over medium heat, stirring occasionally, until the mixture begins to steam. Do not let it boil.
2. **Whisk the Egg Yolks:**
    - In a separate bowl, whisk the egg yolks until smooth.
3. **Temper the Eggs:**
    - Gradually pour about 1 cup of the hot yogurt mixture into the egg yolks, whisking constantly to temper the eggs. Gradually add the tempered egg mixture back into the saucepan with the remaining yogurt mixture, stirring constantly.
4. **Cook the Custard:**
    - Cook the custard over medium-low heat, stirring constantly, until it thickens and coats the back of a spoon, about 8-10 minutes. Remove from heat.
5. **Add Vanilla Extract and Honey (if using):**
    - Stir in the vanilla extract and honey until well combined.
6. **Cool the Custard:**
    - Pour the custard through a fine-mesh sieve into a clean bowl to remove any lumps. Let it cool to room temperature, then cover with plastic wrap, pressing it directly onto the surface of the custard to prevent a skin from forming. Chill in the refrigerator for at least 4 hours or overnight until thoroughly chilled.
7. **Prepare the Figs:**
    - While the custard is chilling, chop the fresh figs into small pieces.

8. **Churn the Ice Cream:**
   - Once chilled, churn the custard in an ice cream maker according to the manufacturer's instructions until it reaches a soft-serve consistency.
9. **Add Chopped Figs:**
   - During the last few minutes of churning, add the chopped figs. Churn until evenly distributed.
10. **Freeze the Ice Cream:**
    - Transfer the churned ice cream into an airtight container, layering with additional chopped figs if desired. Press a piece of parchment paper or plastic wrap directly onto the surface of the ice cream to prevent ice crystals from forming. Freeze for at least 4 hours or until firm.
11. **Serve:**
    - Scoop the Greek Yogurt and Figs Ice Cream into bowls or cones. Enjoy the creamy texture and the sweet, earthy flavor of figs in this delightful frozen dessert!

This Greek Yogurt and Figs Ice Cream offers a balance of creamy yogurt and the natural sweetness of figs, making it a perfect treat for summer or any time you crave a refreshing dessert. Adjust the sweetness by varying the amount of sugar or honey according to your taste preferences. Serve it as a special dessert that will impress with its creamy texture and delightful flavors!

Cucumber Mint Sorbet

Ingredients:

- 2 large cucumbers, peeled and seeded
- 1 cup water
- 1/2 cup sugar
- Juice of 1-2 lemons (depending on taste)
- Zest of 1 lemon
- 1/2 cup fresh mint leaves, packed

Instructions:

1. **Prepare the Cucumbers:**
    - Peel and seed the cucumbers. Cut them into chunks.
2. **Make the Simple Syrup:**
    - In a small saucepan, combine the water and sugar. Heat over medium heat, stirring occasionally, until the sugar is completely dissolved. Remove from heat and let it cool.
3. **Blend Cucumbers and Mint:**
    - In a blender or food processor, puree the cucumbers, fresh mint leaves, lemon zest, and lemon juice until smooth.
4. **Strain the Mixture:**
    - Strain the cucumber and mint puree through a fine-mesh sieve or cheesecloth into a clean bowl to remove any solids. Press gently to extract all the liquid.
5. **Combine and Chill:**
    - Stir the cooled simple syrup into the cucumber-mint mixture. Mix well to combine. Cover the bowl with plastic wrap and refrigerate the mixture until thoroughly chilled, at least 2-3 hours or overnight.
6. **Churn the Sorbet:**
    - Once chilled, pour the cucumber-mint mixture into an ice cream maker and churn according to the manufacturer's instructions until it reaches a slushy consistency.
7. **Freeze the Sorbet:**
    - Transfer the churned sorbet into an airtight container. Press a piece of parchment paper or plastic wrap directly onto the surface of the sorbet to prevent ice crystals from forming. Freeze for an additional 2-3 hours, or until firm.
8. **Serve:**

- - Scoop the Cucumber Mint Sorbet into bowls or cones. Garnish with a sprig of fresh mint or a slice of cucumber for an extra touch. Enjoy the cool and refreshing flavor of this unique sorbet!

This Cucumber Mint Sorbet is perfect for hot summer days, offering a light and refreshing dessert with a blend of cucumber's coolness and mint's aromatic freshness. Adjust the sweetness and tartness by varying the amount of sugar and lemon juice according to your taste preferences. Serve it as a palate cleanser between courses or as a delightful dessert that will impress with its unique flavors!

Lemon Ouzo Ice Cream

Ingredients:

- 2 cups heavy cream
- 1 cup whole milk
- 3/4 cup sugar
- Zest of 2 lemons
- 1/2 cup fresh lemon juice (about 4-5 lemons)
- 4 egg yolks
- Pinch of salt
- 1/4 cup ouzo (Greek anise-flavored liqueur)
- 1 teaspoon vanilla extract

Instructions:

1. **Prepare the Custard:**
    - In a medium saucepan, combine the heavy cream, whole milk, sugar, and lemon zest. Heat over medium heat, stirring occasionally, until the mixture begins to steam. Do not let it boil.
2. **Whisk the Egg Yolks:**
    - In a separate bowl, whisk the egg yolks until smooth.
3. **Temper the Eggs:**
    - Gradually pour about 1 cup of the hot cream mixture into the egg yolks, whisking constantly to temper the eggs. Gradually add the tempered egg mixture back into the saucepan with the remaining cream mixture, stirring constantly.
4. **Cook the Custard:**
    - Cook the custard over medium-low heat, stirring constantly, until it thickens and coats the back of a spoon, about 8-10 minutes. Remove from heat.
5. **Add Lemon Juice, Ouzo, and Vanilla Extract:**
    - Stir in the fresh lemon juice, ouzo, and vanilla extract until well combined.
6. **Cool the Custard:**
    - Pour the custard through a fine-mesh sieve into a clean bowl to remove any lumps and the lemon zest. Let it cool to room temperature, then cover with plastic wrap, pressing it directly onto the surface of the custard to prevent a skin from forming. Chill in the refrigerator for at least 4 hours or overnight until thoroughly chilled.
7. **Churn the Ice Cream:**

- Once chilled, churn the custard in an ice cream maker according to the manufacturer's instructions until it reaches a soft-serve consistency.

8. **Freeze the Ice Cream:**
   - Transfer the churned ice cream into an airtight container. Press a piece of parchment paper or plastic wrap directly onto the surface of the ice cream to prevent ice crystals from forming. Freeze for at least 4 hours or until firm.
9. **Serve:**
   - Scoop the Lemon Ouzo Ice Cream into bowls or cones. Garnish with a twist of lemon zest or a small sprig of fresh mint if desired. Enjoy the refreshing and aromatic flavors of this unique frozen dessert!

This Lemon Ouzo Ice Cream offers a delightful blend of citrusy lemon and the subtle anise notes of ouzo, creating a refreshing and aromatic treat. Adjust the sweetness and tartness by varying the amount of sugar and lemon juice according to your taste preferences. Serve it as a special dessert that will impress with its unique flavors!

Melon Sorbet

Ingredients:

- 1 medium ripe melon (cantaloupe, honeydew, or whichever you prefer)
- 1/2 cup granulated sugar (adjust according to the sweetness of the melon)
- 1/4 cup water
- 1-2 tablespoons fresh lemon juice (optional, to enhance the flavor)

Instructions:

1. **Prepare the Melon:** Cut the melon in half, remove the seeds, and scoop out the flesh. Cut the flesh into chunks.
2. **Make the Simple Syrup:** In a small saucepan, combine the sugar and water. Heat over medium heat, stirring occasionally, until the sugar completely dissolves. Remove from heat and let it cool to room temperature.
3. **Blend the Sorbet Base:** In a blender or food processor, combine the melon chunks and simple syrup. Blend until smooth. Add fresh lemon juice, if using, and blend again briefly to combine.
4. **Chill the Mixture:** Transfer the sorbet mixture into a bowl or container, cover, and refrigerate until thoroughly chilled, at least 2 hours or overnight.
5. **Churn the Sorbet:** Once chilled, pour the mixture into an ice cream maker and churn according to the manufacturer's instructions until it reaches a sorbet consistency.
6. **Serve or Store:** Serve immediately for a soft sorbet texture, or transfer to a container and freeze for a few hours for a firmer texture.
7. **Enjoy:** Scoop into bowls or cones and enjoy the refreshing taste of homemade melon sorbet!

Feel free to adjust the sweetness and lemon juice according to your taste preferences and the natural sweetness of the melon you choose.

Apricot and Honey Ice Cream

Ingredients:

- 1 pound (about 450g) ripe apricots, pitted and chopped
- 1/2 cup honey
- 1 cup whole milk
- 1 cup heavy cream
- 1/2 cup granulated sugar
- 4 large egg yolks
- 1 teaspoon vanilla extract

Instructions:

1. **Prepare the Apricots:** In a saucepan, combine the chopped apricots and honey. Cook over medium heat, stirring occasionally, until the apricots are soft and the mixture is syrupy, about 10-15 minutes. Remove from heat and let it cool slightly.
2. **Blend the Apricots:** Transfer the cooked apricot mixture to a blender or food processor. Blend until smooth. Set aside.
3. **Prepare the Ice Cream Base:** In a medium saucepan, combine the milk, heavy cream, and granulated sugar. Heat over medium heat, stirring occasionally, until the sugar is dissolved and the mixture is hot but not boiling.
4. **Temper the Egg Yolks:** In a separate bowl, whisk the egg yolks. Gradually whisk in about 1/2 cup of the hot milk mixture to temper the yolks. Then, slowly whisk the tempered yolks back into the saucepan with the remaining milk mixture.
5. **Cook the Custard:** Cook the mixture over medium heat, stirring constantly, until it thickens enough to coat the back of a spoon (around 170-175°F or 75-80°C). Do not let it boil.
6. **Combine with Apricot Puree:** Remove the custard from heat and whisk in the apricot puree and vanilla extract until well combined.
7. **Chill the Mixture:** Strain the mixture through a fine mesh sieve into a clean bowl to remove any solids. Cover and refrigerate until completely chilled, at least 4 hours or overnight.
8. **Churn the Ice Cream:** Once chilled, pour the mixture into an ice cream maker and churn according to the manufacturer's instructions until it reaches a soft-serve consistency.
9. **Freeze:** Transfer the ice cream to a container, press a piece of parchment paper or plastic wrap directly on the surface to prevent ice crystals from forming, and freeze until firm, about 4 hours or overnight.

10. **Serve and Enjoy:** Scoop the apricot and honey ice cream into bowls or cones, garnish with fresh apricot slices or a drizzle of honey if desired, and enjoy!

This ice cream captures the natural sweetness of apricots and the richness of honey, making it a perfect summer treat.

Rose Petal Ice Cream

Ingredients:

- 2 cups heavy cream
- 1 cup whole milk
- 1/2 cup granulated sugar
- 1/4 cup dried rose petals (culinary grade, unsprayed)
- 4 large egg yolks
- 1 teaspoon rose water (adjust to taste)
- Pink food coloring (optional)

Instructions:

1. **Infuse the Cream and Milk:**
   - In a saucepan, combine the heavy cream, whole milk, granulated sugar, and dried rose petals.
   - Heat over medium-low heat, stirring occasionally, until the mixture is hot and just begins to simmer. Do not boil.
   - Remove from heat, cover the saucepan, and let the mixture steep for about 30 minutes to infuse the flavors of the rose petals into the cream.
2. **Prepare the Egg Yolks:**
   - In a separate bowl, whisk the egg yolks until smooth.
3. **Temper the Eggs:**
   - After the cream mixture has steeped, strain it through a fine mesh sieve into a clean saucepan to remove the rose petals.
   - Reheat the infused cream mixture over medium heat until it is hot but not boiling.
   - Gradually pour a small amount of the hot cream mixture into the bowl with the egg yolks, whisking constantly. This tempers the eggs and prevents them from scrambling.
4. **Combine and Cook the Custard:**
   - Pour the tempered egg mixture back into the saucepan with the remaining hot cream mixture, whisking constantly.
   - Cook the mixture over medium heat, stirring constantly with a wooden spoon or spatula, until it thickens enough to coat the back of the spoon (around 170-175°F or 75-80°C). The custard should be smooth and creamy.
5. **Strain and Chill:**

- Remove the custard from heat and immediately strain it through a fine mesh sieve into a clean bowl to remove any cooked egg bits or solids.
- Stir in the rose water. Add a drop or two of pink food coloring if you desire a more vibrant color. Mix well.

6. **Chill the Mixture:**
   - Cover the bowl with plastic wrap, pressing it directly onto the surface of the custard to prevent a skin from forming.
   - Refrigerate until completely chilled, at least 4 hours or overnight.

7. **Churn the Ice Cream:**
   - Once chilled, pour the rose petal custard into an ice cream maker and churn according to the manufacturer's instructions until it reaches a soft-serve consistency.

8. **Freeze:**
   - Transfer the churned ice cream to a container. Press a piece of parchment paper or plastic wrap directly onto the surface to prevent ice crystals from forming.
   - Freeze until firm, about 4 hours or overnight.

9. **Serve and Enjoy:**
   - Scoop the rose petal ice cream into bowls or cones, garnish with edible rose petals or a sprinkle of dried rose petals for a lovely presentation, and enjoy the delicate floral flavors!

This rose petal ice cream is sure to impress with its unique flavor and beautiful appearance. Adjust the amount of rose water to suit your preference for the intensity of the rose flavor.

Watermelon Mint Sorbet

Ingredients:

- 4 cups cubed seedless watermelon
- 1/2 cup granulated sugar (adjust according to the sweetness of the watermelon)
- 1/4 cup fresh mint leaves, packed
- 1/4 cup water
- 1-2 tablespoons fresh lime juice

Instructions:

1. **Prepare the Watermelon:**
   - Cut the watermelon into cubes, discarding any seeds. You should have about 4 cups of cubed watermelon.
2. **Make the Mint Syrup:**
   - In a small saucepan, combine the sugar, fresh mint leaves, and water.
   - Heat over medium heat, stirring occasionally, until the sugar is completely dissolved and the mixture comes to a simmer.
   - Remove from heat and let the mint steep in the syrup for about 10-15 minutes to infuse the flavor.
3. **Blend the Ingredients:**
   - In a blender or food processor, combine the cubed watermelon and the mint syrup (strained to remove the mint leaves).
   - Add fresh lime juice to taste. Blend until the mixture is smooth and well combined.
4. **Chill the Mixture:**
   - Pour the watermelon mixture into a bowl or container through a fine mesh sieve to remove any pulp or solids.
   - Cover and refrigerate the mixture until thoroughly chilled, at least 2 hours or overnight.
5. **Churn the Sorbet:**
   - Once chilled, pour the watermelon mixture into an ice cream maker and churn according to the manufacturer's instructions until it reaches a sorbet consistency.
6. **Freeze:**
   - Transfer the churned sorbet into a freezer-safe container. Cover the surface with parchment paper or plastic wrap to prevent ice crystals from forming.
   - Freeze for a few hours until firm.

7. **Serve and Enjoy:**
    - Scoop the watermelon mint sorbet into bowls or cones. Garnish with fresh mint leaves or a wedge of lime if desired.
    - Enjoy this refreshing and fruity sorbet as a cooling dessert!

This watermelon mint sorbet captures the sweet essence of watermelon with a hint of mint, making it a perfect treat for summer gatherings or just to enjoy on a sunny day. Adjust the sweetness and mint flavor according to your taste preference.

Mastic Rose Ice Cream

Ingredients:

- 2 cups heavy cream
- 1 cup whole milk
- 3/4 cup granulated sugar
- 1 tablespoon mastic resin crystals (available at Middle Eastern grocery stores or online)
- 4 large egg yolks
- 1-2 tablespoons rose water (adjust to taste)
- Pink or red food coloring (optional, for a more vibrant color)

Instructions:

1. **Prepare the Mastic:**
    - Crush the mastic resin crystals into a fine powder using a mortar and pestle or by placing them in a plastic bag and gently crushing with a rolling pin. Set aside.
2. **Make the Ice Cream Base:**
    - In a saucepan, combine the heavy cream, whole milk, and granulated sugar. Heat over medium heat, stirring occasionally, until the mixture is hot and just begins to simmer (do not boil).
3. **Infuse with Mastic:**
    - Add the crushed mastic resin to the hot cream mixture. Stir continuously until the mastic is completely dissolved and the mixture is well combined. Remove from heat.
4. **Temper the Egg Yolks:**
    - In a separate bowl, whisk the egg yolks until smooth. Gradually whisk in about 1/2 cup of the hot cream mixture into the egg yolks, whisking constantly. This tempers the eggs and prevents them from scrambling.
5. **Combine and Cook the Custard:**
    - Pour the tempered egg mixture back into the saucepan with the remaining hot cream mixture, whisking constantly.
    - Cook the mixture over medium heat, stirring constantly with a wooden spoon or spatula, until it thickens enough to coat the back of the spoon (around 170-175°F or 75-80°C). The custard should be smooth and creamy.
6. **Strain and Chill:**

- Remove the custard from heat and immediately strain it through a fine mesh sieve into a clean bowl to remove any cooked egg bits or solids.
- Stir in the rose water. Add a drop or two of pink or red food coloring if desired for a more vibrant color. Mix well.

7. **Chill the Mixture:**
   - Cover the bowl with plastic wrap, pressing it directly onto the surface of the custard to prevent a skin from forming.
   - Refrigerate until completely chilled, at least 4 hours or overnight.

8. **Churn the Ice Cream:**
   - Once chilled, pour the mastic rose custard into an ice cream maker and churn according to the manufacturer's instructions until it reaches a soft-serve consistency.

9. **Freeze:**
   - Transfer the churned ice cream to a container. Press a piece of parchment paper or plastic wrap directly onto the surface to prevent ice crystals from forming.
   - Freeze until firm, about 4 hours or overnight.

10. **Serve and Enjoy:**

- Scoop the mastic rose ice cream into bowls or cones, garnish with edible rose petals or a sprinkle of crushed mastic if desired, and enjoy the unique flavors of this aromatic dessert!

This mastic rose ice cream is a delightful blend of floral and slightly resinous notes, perfect for those who enjoy exotic and distinctive flavors in their desserts. Adjust the amount of rose water and mastic according to your taste preferences.

Almond and Honey Ice Cream

Ingredients:

- 1 cup whole milk
- 2 cups heavy cream
- 3/4 cup granulated sugar
- 1/2 cup almond paste or finely ground almonds
- 4 large egg yolks
- 1/4 cup honey
- 1 teaspoon almond extract
- 1/2 cup toasted almonds, chopped (optional, for texture)

Instructions:

1. **Prepare the Almond Base:**
   - In a saucepan, combine the whole milk, heavy cream, and granulated sugar. Heat over medium heat, stirring occasionally, until the mixture is hot and just begins to simmer (do not boil).
2. **Add Almond Paste or Ground Almonds:**
   - Stir in the almond paste or finely ground almonds until well combined and dissolved into the cream mixture. If using almond paste, ensure it melts and blends smoothly.
3. **Temper the Egg Yolks:**
   - In a separate bowl, whisk the egg yolks until smooth. Gradually whisk in about 1/2 cup of the hot cream mixture into the egg yolks, whisking constantly. This tempers the eggs and prevents them from scrambling.
4. **Combine and Cook the Custard:**
   - Pour the tempered egg mixture back into the saucepan with the remaining hot cream mixture, whisking constantly.
   - Cook the mixture over medium heat, stirring constantly with a wooden spoon or spatula, until it thickens enough to coat the back of the spoon (around 170-175°F or 75-80°C). The custard should be smooth and creamy.
5. **Add Honey and Almond Extract:**
   - Remove the custard from heat and immediately stir in the honey and almond extract. Mix until well combined.
6. **Chill the Mixture:**
   - Strain the custard through a fine mesh sieve into a clean bowl to remove any cooked egg bits or solids.

- Cover the bowl with plastic wrap, pressing it directly onto the surface of the custard to prevent a skin from forming.
- Refrigerate until completely chilled, at least 4 hours or overnight.

7. **Churn the Ice Cream:**
   - Once chilled, pour the almond and honey custard into an ice cream maker and churn according to the manufacturer's instructions until it reaches a soft-serve consistency.

8. **Add Toasted Almonds (Optional):**
   - If desired, stir in the chopped toasted almonds during the last few minutes of churning for added texture and nutty flavor.

9. **Freeze:**
   - Transfer the churned ice cream to a container. Press a piece of parchment paper or plastic wrap directly onto the surface to prevent ice crystals from forming.
   - Freeze until firm, about 4 hours or overnight.

10. **Serve and Enjoy:**

- Scoop the almond and honey ice cream into bowls or cones. Garnish with extra toasted almonds if desired, and savor the delicious combination of almond flavor with the natural sweetness of honey!

This almond and honey ice cream is creamy, nutty, and subtly sweet, making it a wonderful dessert for almond lovers or anyone looking to enjoy a rich and flavorful treat. Adjust the sweetness level by varying the amount of honey according to your preference.

Pear and Ginger Ice Cream

Ingredients:

- 3 ripe pears, peeled, cored, and chopped
- 1 tablespoon lemon juice
- 1/2 cup granulated sugar
- 1 cup whole milk
- 2 cups heavy cream
- 4 large egg yolks
- 1/4 cup crystallized ginger, finely chopped
- 1 teaspoon vanilla extract

Instructions:

1. **Prepare the Pears:**
    - In a saucepan, combine the chopped pears, lemon juice, and granulated sugar. Cook over medium heat, stirring occasionally, until the pears are soft and tender, about 10-15 minutes. Mash the pears slightly with a fork or potato masher. Let the mixture cool slightly.
2. **Blend the Pear Mixture:**
    - Transfer the cooked pear mixture to a blender or food processor. Blend until smooth. Set aside.
3. **Prepare the Ice Cream Base:**
    - In a saucepan, combine the whole milk and heavy cream. Heat over medium heat, stirring occasionally, until the mixture is hot and just begins to simmer (do not boil).
4. **Temper the Egg Yolks:**
    - In a separate bowl, whisk the egg yolks until smooth. Gradually whisk in about 1/2 cup of the hot cream mixture into the egg yolks, whisking constantly. This tempers the eggs and prevents them from scrambling.
5. **Combine and Cook the Custard:**
    - Pour the tempered egg mixture back into the saucepan with the remaining hot cream mixture, whisking constantly.
    - Cook the mixture over medium heat, stirring constantly with a wooden spoon or spatula, until it thickens enough to coat the back of the spoon (around 170-175°F or 75-80°C). The custard should be smooth and creamy.
6. **Combine Pear Puree and Ginger:**

- Remove the custard from heat. Stir in the blended pear mixture, finely chopped crystallized ginger, and vanilla extract until well combined.

7. **Chill the Mixture:**
   - Strain the custard through a fine mesh sieve into a clean bowl to remove any cooked egg bits or solids.
   - Cover the bowl with plastic wrap, pressing it directly onto the surface of the custard to prevent a skin from forming.
   - Refrigerate until completely chilled, at least 4 hours or overnight.

8. **Churn the Ice Cream:**
   - Once chilled, pour the pear and ginger custard into an ice cream maker and churn according to the manufacturer's instructions until it reaches a soft-serve consistency.

9. **Freeze:**
   - Transfer the churned ice cream to a container. Press a piece of parchment paper or plastic wrap directly onto the surface to prevent ice crystals from forming.
   - Freeze until firm, about 4 hours or overnight.

10. **Serve and Enjoy:**

- Scoop the pear and ginger ice cream into bowls or cones. Garnish with a slice of fresh pear or a sprinkle of chopped crystallized ginger if desired.
- Enjoy the creamy texture and balanced flavors of pear and ginger in this delicious homemade ice cream!

This pear and ginger ice cream is a delightful blend of sweet and spicy flavors, perfect for a refreshing dessert on a warm day or as a special treat any time of year. Adjust the amount of ginger according to your taste preference for a stronger or milder ginger flavor.

Mastic Pistachio Ice Cream

Ingredients:

- 2 cups heavy cream
- 1 cup whole milk
- 3/4 cup granulated sugar
- 1 tablespoon mastic resin crystals (available at Middle Eastern grocery stores or online)
- 4 large egg yolks
- 1 teaspoon vanilla extract
- 1 cup shelled pistachios, toasted and chopped

Instructions:

1. **Prepare the Mastic Infusion:**
    - Crush the mastic resin crystals into a fine powder using a mortar and pestle or by placing them in a plastic bag and gently crushing with a rolling pin.
2. **Make the Ice Cream Base:**
    - In a saucepan, combine the heavy cream, whole milk, and granulated sugar. Heat over medium heat, stirring occasionally, until the mixture is hot and just begins to simmer (do not boil).
3. **Add Mastic and Pistachios:**
    - Stir in the crushed mastic resin into the hot cream mixture, stirring continuously until it is completely dissolved and well combined.
    - Add the chopped pistachios to the cream mixture. Stir well.
4. **Temper the Egg Yolks:**
    - In a separate bowl, whisk the egg yolks until smooth. Gradually whisk in about 1/2 cup of the hot cream mixture into the egg yolks, whisking constantly. This tempers the eggs and prevents them from scrambling.
5. **Combine and Cook the Custard:**
    - Pour the tempered egg mixture back into the saucepan with the remaining hot cream mixture, whisking constantly.
    - Cook the mixture over medium heat, stirring constantly with a wooden spoon or spatula, until it thickens enough to coat the back of the spoon (around 170-175°F or 75-80°C). The custard should be smooth and creamy.
6. **Strain and Chill:**

- Remove the custard from heat and immediately strain it through a fine mesh sieve into a clean bowl to remove any cooked egg bits or solids.
- Stir in the vanilla extract. Mix well.

7. **Chill the Mixture:**
   - Cover the bowl with plastic wrap, pressing it directly onto the surface of the custard to prevent a skin from forming.
   - Refrigerate until completely chilled, at least 4 hours or overnight.
8. **Churn the Ice Cream:**
   - Once chilled, pour the mastic pistachio custard into an ice cream maker and churn according to the manufacturer's instructions until it reaches a soft-serve consistency.
9. **Freeze:**
   - Transfer the churned ice cream to a container. Press a piece of parchment paper or plastic wrap directly onto the surface to prevent ice crystals from forming.
   - Freeze until firm, about 4 hours or overnight.
10. **Serve and Enjoy:**

- Scoop the mastic pistachio ice cream into bowls or cones. Garnish with additional chopped pistachios if desired.
- Enjoy the creamy texture and unique flavors of mastic and pistachios in this delicious homemade ice cream!

This mastic pistachio ice cream is a wonderful blend of nutty pistachio flavor with a subtle hint of resinous mastic, making it a delightful and exotic dessert that's sure to impress. Adjust the amount of mastic according to your preference for its distinct flavor.

Olive Oil and Sea Salt Ice Cream

Ingredients:

- 2 cups heavy cream
- 1 cup whole milk
- 3/4 cup granulated sugar
- 1/2 cup good quality extra virgin olive oil
- 4 large egg yolks
- 1 teaspoon vanilla extract
- 1/2 teaspoon sea salt (adjust to taste)
- Additional sea salt flakes, for garnish (optional)

Instructions:

1. **Prepare the Ice Cream Base:**
    - In a saucepan, combine the heavy cream, whole milk, and granulated sugar. Heat over medium heat, stirring occasionally, until the mixture is hot and just begins to simmer (do not boil).
2. **Add Olive Oil:**
    - Stir in the extra virgin olive oil into the hot cream mixture. Mix well until the olive oil is fully incorporated.
3. **Temper the Egg Yolks:**
    - In a separate bowl, whisk the egg yolks until smooth. Gradually whisk in about 1/2 cup of the hot cream mixture into the egg yolks, whisking constantly. This tempers the eggs and prevents them from scrambling.
4. **Combine and Cook the Custard:**
    - Pour the tempered egg mixture back into the saucepan with the remaining hot cream mixture, whisking constantly.
    - Cook the mixture over medium heat, stirring constantly with a wooden spoon or spatula, until it thickens enough to coat the back of the spoon (around 170-175°F or 75-80°C). The custard should be smooth and creamy.
5. **Add Vanilla and Sea Salt:**
    - Remove the custard from heat and stir in the vanilla extract and sea salt. Mix until well combined.
6. **Chill the Mixture:**
    - Strain the custard through a fine mesh sieve into a clean bowl to remove any cooked egg bits or solids.

- Cover the bowl with plastic wrap, pressing it directly onto the surface of the custard to prevent a skin from forming.
- Refrigerate until completely chilled, at least 4 hours or overnight.

7. **Churn the Ice Cream:**
   - Once chilled, pour the olive oil and sea salt custard into an ice cream maker and churn according to the manufacturer's instructions until it reaches a soft-serve consistency.

8. **Freeze:**
   - Transfer the churned ice cream to a container. Press a piece of parchment paper or plastic wrap directly onto the surface to prevent ice crystals from forming.
   - Freeze until firm, about 4 hours or overnight.

9. **Serve and Garnish:**
   - Scoop the olive oil and sea salt ice cream into bowls or cones. If desired, garnish with a sprinkle of sea salt flakes for added texture and flavor contrast.

10. **Enjoy:**
- Enjoy the unique and sophisticated flavors of olive oil and sea salt in this creamy and delicious homemade ice cream!

This olive oil and sea salt ice cream is a wonderful choice for those looking to explore savory-sweet combinations in desserts. The olive oil adds a silky texture and subtle flavor, while the sea salt enhances the overall taste experience. Adjust the amount of sea salt according to your preference for a more or less pronounced salty flavor.

Lemon Thyme Sorbet

Ingredients:

- 1 cup water
- 1 cup granulated sugar
- Zest of 2 lemons
- 1/2 cup freshly squeezed lemon juice (about 3-4 lemons)
- 2 tablespoons fresh thyme leaves, chopped
- Optional: 1-2 tablespoons vodka (helps keep the sorbet soft)

Instructions:

1. **Make the Simple Syrup:**
   - In a saucepan, combine the water, granulated sugar, and lemon zest. Heat over medium heat, stirring occasionally, until the sugar is completely dissolved. This will make a simple syrup infused with lemon zest.
2. **Infuse with Thyme:**
   - Remove the simple syrup from heat and stir in the chopped fresh thyme leaves. Let the mixture steep for about 15-20 minutes to infuse the thyme flavor into the syrup. Strain the syrup through a fine mesh sieve to remove the thyme leaves and lemon zest.
3. **Combine Lemon Juice:**
   - Stir in the freshly squeezed lemon juice into the infused simple syrup. Mix well.
4. **Optional: Add Vodka (if using):**
   - Stir in 1-2 tablespoons of vodka into the lemon thyme mixture. This helps keep the sorbet soft and scoopable when frozen.
5. **Chill the Mixture:**
   - Transfer the lemon thyme mixture to a container or bowl. Cover and refrigerate until completely chilled, at least 2-3 hours or overnight.
6. **Churn the Sorbet:**
   - Once chilled, pour the lemon thyme mixture into an ice cream maker and churn according to the manufacturer's instructions until it reaches a sorbet consistency.
7. **Freeze:**
   - Transfer the churned sorbet into a freezer-safe container. Press a piece of parchment paper or plastic wrap directly onto the surface to prevent ice crystals from forming.
   - Freeze until firm, about 4 hours or overnight.

8. **Serve and Enjoy:**
    - Scoop the lemon thyme sorbet into bowls or cones. Garnish with a sprig of fresh thyme or a twist of lemon zest if desired.
    - Enjoy the refreshing and herbaceous flavors of lemon thyme in this delightful sorbet!

This lemon thyme sorbet is perfect for cleansing the palate after a meal or as a light and refreshing dessert on a hot day. The combination of citrusy lemon and aromatic thyme makes for a unique and sophisticated flavor profile. Adjust the sweetness and tartness by varying the amount of sugar and lemon juice according to your taste preference.

Lavender and Honey Ice Cream

Ingredients:

- 2 cups heavy cream
- 1 cup whole milk
- 1/2 cup honey
- 1/4 cup dried culinary lavender buds
- 1/2 cup granulated sugar
- 4 large egg yolks
- 1 teaspoon vanilla extract

Instructions:

1. **Infuse the Cream and Milk:**
     - In a saucepan, combine the heavy cream, whole milk, honey, and dried lavender buds. Heat over medium-low heat, stirring occasionally, until the mixture is hot and just begins to simmer. Do not boil.
     - Remove from heat, cover the saucepan, and let the mixture steep for about 20-30 minutes to infuse the flavors of the lavender into the cream.
2. **Strain the Mixture:**
     - After steeping, strain the lavender-infused cream mixture through a fine mesh sieve into a clean saucepan to remove the lavender buds. Press down on the lavender buds to extract all the infused flavors.
3. **Prepare the Egg Yolks:**
     - In a separate bowl, whisk the egg yolks and granulated sugar until smooth and creamy.
4. **Temper the Eggs:**
     - Gradually pour a small amount of the hot lavender-infused cream mixture into the bowl with the egg yolks, whisking constantly. This process tempers the eggs and prevents them from curdling.
5. **Combine and Cook the Custard:**
     - Pour the tempered egg mixture back into the saucepan with the remaining lavender-infused cream mixture. Cook over medium heat, stirring constantly with a wooden spoon or spatula, until the mixture thickens enough to coat the back of the spoon (around 170-175°F or 75-80°C). The custard should be smooth and creamy.
6. **Strain and Chill:**
     - Remove the custard from heat and immediately strain it through a fine mesh sieve into a clean bowl to remove any cooked egg bits or solids.

- Stir in the vanilla extract. Mix well.
7. **Chill the Mixture:**
    - Cover the bowl with plastic wrap, pressing it directly onto the surface of the custard to prevent a skin from forming.
    - Refrigerate until completely chilled, at least 4 hours or overnight.
8. **Churn the Ice Cream:**
    - Once chilled, pour the lavender and honey custard into an ice cream maker and churn according to the manufacturer's instructions until it reaches a soft-serve consistency.
9. **Freeze:**
    - Transfer the churned ice cream to a container. Press a piece of parchment paper or plastic wrap directly onto the surface to prevent ice crystals from forming.
    - Freeze until firm, about 4 hours or overnight.
10. **Serve and Enjoy:**
- Scoop the lavender and honey ice cream into bowls or cones. Garnish with a sprinkle of dried lavender buds or fresh lavender flowers if desired.
- Enjoy the delicate floral flavors and creamy texture of this homemade lavender and honey ice cream!

This lavender and honey ice cream is a lovely treat, perfect for those who enjoy floral-infused desserts. Adjust the amount of honey and lavender according to your taste preference for sweetness and intensity of lavender flavor.

Greek Yogurt and Honey Sorbet

Ingredients:

- 2 cups Greek yogurt (full-fat for creamier texture)
- 1/2 cup honey (adjust to taste)
- 1/2 cup water
- 1/4 cup fresh lemon juice (about 2 lemons)
- Zest of 1 lemon (optional, for extra flavor)

Instructions:

1. **Prepare the Simple Syrup:**
    - In a small saucepan, combine the honey and water. Heat over medium heat, stirring occasionally, until the honey is completely dissolved and the mixture forms a syrup. Remove from heat and let it cool to room temperature.
2. **Mix the Sorbet Base:**
    - In a large bowl, whisk together the Greek yogurt, cooled honey syrup, fresh lemon juice, and lemon zest (if using). Mix until smooth and well combined.
3. **Chill the Mixture:**
    - Cover the bowl with plastic wrap, pressing it directly onto the surface of the yogurt mixture to prevent a skin from forming.
    - Refrigerate the mixture until thoroughly chilled, at least 2-3 hours or overnight.
4. **Churn the Sorbet:**
    - Once chilled, pour the yogurt and honey mixture into an ice cream maker and churn according to the manufacturer's instructions until it reaches a sorbet consistency. This typically takes about 20-25 minutes.
5. **Freeze:**
    - Transfer the churned sorbet into a freezer-safe container. Press a piece of parchment paper or plastic wrap directly onto the surface to prevent ice crystals from forming.
    - Freeze the sorbet until firm, about 3-4 hours or overnight.
6. **Serve and Enjoy:**
    - Scoop the Greek yogurt and honey sorbet into bowls or cones. Garnish with a drizzle of honey or fresh berries if desired.
    - Enjoy the creamy and tangy sweetness of this delightful Greek yogurt and honey sorbet!

This sorbet is perfect for a light and refreshing dessert, combining the smoothness of Greek yogurt with the floral sweetness of honey. Adjust the amount of honey according to your taste preference, and feel free to add more lemon zest for an extra zing of citrus flavor.

Mastelo and Cinnamon Ice Cream

Ingredients:

- 2 cups heavy cream
- 1 cup whole milk
- 3/4 cup granulated sugar
- 8 ounces mastelo cheese, finely grated or crumbled (you can substitute with a mild, salty cheese like kefalotyri or kefalograviera)
- 4 large egg yolks
- 1 teaspoon vanilla extract
- 1 teaspoon ground cinnamon
- Pinch of salt

Instructions:

1. **Prepare the Ice Cream Base:**
   - In a saucepan, combine the heavy cream, whole milk, and granulated sugar. Heat over medium heat, stirring occasionally, until the mixture is hot and just begins to simmer (do not boil).
2. **Add Mastelo Cheese and Cinnamon:**
   - Stir in the finely grated or crumbled mastelo cheese and ground cinnamon into the hot cream mixture. Mix well until the cheese is fully incorporated and melted into the cream.
3. **Temper the Egg Yolks:**
   - In a separate bowl, whisk the egg yolks until smooth. Gradually whisk in about 1/2 cup of the hot cream mixture into the egg yolks, whisking constantly. This tempers the eggs and prevents them from scrambling.
4. **Combine and Cook the Custard:**
   - Pour the tempered egg mixture back into the saucepan with the remaining hot cream mixture, whisking constantly.
   - Cook the mixture over medium heat, stirring constantly with a wooden spoon or spatula, until it thickens enough to coat the back of the spoon (around 170-175°F or 75-80°C). The custard should be smooth and creamy.
5. **Add Vanilla and Salt:**
   - Remove the custard from heat and stir in the vanilla extract and a pinch of salt. Mix until well combined.
6. **Chill the Mixture:**

- Strain the custard through a fine mesh sieve into a clean bowl to remove any cooked egg bits or solids.
- Cover the bowl with plastic wrap, pressing it directly onto the surface of the custard to prevent a skin from forming.
- Refrigerate until completely chilled, at least 4 hours or overnight.

7. **Churn the Ice Cream:**
    - Once chilled, pour the mastelo and cinnamon custard into an ice cream maker and churn according to the manufacturer's instructions until it reaches a soft-serve consistency.
8. **Freeze:**
    - Transfer the churned ice cream to a container. Press a piece of parchment paper or plastic wrap directly onto the surface to prevent ice crystals from forming.
    - Freeze until firm, about 4 hours or overnight.
9. **Serve and Enjoy:**
    - Scoop the mastelo and cinnamon ice cream into bowls or cones. Garnish with a sprinkle of ground cinnamon or a small piece of mastelo cheese if desired.
    - Enjoy the savory-sweet flavors and creamy texture of this unique ice cream creation!

This mastelo and cinnamon ice cream offers a savory twist on traditional sweet desserts, perfect for those who enjoy exploring new flavor combinations. Adjust the amount of cinnamon according to your taste preference for a more pronounced or subtle spice flavor.